Abstract Concepts
of
DRAWING

Abstract Concepts
of
DRAWING

Written and compiled by
Robert Paterson

VAN NOSTRAND REINHOLD COMPANY
NEW YORK CINCINNATI TORONTO LONDON MELBOURNE

I wish to thank all those who have so willingly allowed their work to be used in this book, Marion for her patience and understanding, and David Cavanagh for his clear editorial assistance.

First published in the United States in 1983
Copyright© 1981 by Robert A. Paterson
Library of Congress Catalog Card Number 82-62077
ISBN 0-442-27427-0

Printed in the United States of America

Van Nostrand Reinhold Company Inc.
135 West 50th Street
New York, New York 10020

Van Nostrand Reinhold Australia Pty. Ltd.
480 Latrobe Street
Melbourne, Victoria 3000, Australia

Van Nostrand Reinhold Company Limited
Molly Millars Lane
Wokingham, Berkshire, England RG11 2PY

Canadian edition published 1981 by Robert A. Paterson

16 15 14 13 12 11 10 9 8 7 6 5 4 3 2 1

CONTENTS

1 Introduction

7 Lines

27 Shapes

41 Form

67 Texture

83 Space and Perspective

103 Information

119 Composition

145 Expression

155 Idioms and Ideas

167 Index

Drawings which are not credited
have been supplied by the author.

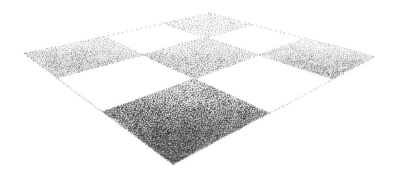

Introduction

Drawing relates to all creative activities which combine Visual elements in a meaningful way. Even when we choose clothes to wear, select a car, or set the table for a special occasion, we are dealing with Visual concerns, or Abstract Concepts. When we want something to be attractive or otherwise visually interesting, some aspect of drawing will be involved.

Drawing often serves as the planning or 'thinking' stage for other works, or as an enjoyable hobby. It can be the Information Gatherer, or a means of becoming involved with a setting such as a landscape or exotic street scene. It can be a game. Drawing can be a means of expressing Ideas in an endless number of ways, and is therefore not confined to limited functions. Because it relates to so many things, and can play so many roles, drawing must be considered the major element in the area of Visual Communication.

Never having been an activity simply devoted to mirroring Nature, Art is a messenger conveying Ideas through a means of Expression similar to Music or Dance. We understand that all body movements are not Dance, nor is all noise Music. Similarly all markings on a surface are not Art. Movement, sounds, and images, must communicate something special which appeals to the senses through the way in which they are presented.

The raw materials of Visual Expression have been around since ancient man first realized that drawn images could evoke emotional responses and add meaning to his existence, but only gradually have we come to appreciate them. These elements are defined and presented in this book as Abstract Concepts and they are understood to be aside from the subject matter. They help provide the Visual Meaning of a work of Art, while the subject supplies the Literal Meaning. The true essence of a work lies in its Visual Meaning, this being the part which cannot be described in words, and what creativity is all about.

The Abstract Concepts of drawing are considered here to be Line, Shape, Form, Texture, Space (and Perspective), Information, Composition, and Expression. Each one possesses individual virtues which must be appreciated if it is to be used wisely and effectively. The additional Concept of Colour would embrace the field of painting, but is not included here because drawing basically explores the potential of using only one contrasting material such as black or brown, etc. In any case, black has often been considered to be the 'most essential Colour' due to its basic honesty.

An Abstract Concept represents the artist's Visual Idea and provides the structure necessary for a drawing to have an energy capable of seducing the viewer into contemplation of it. If, for example, a drawing displays an expressive use of Line as its main attracting force, then the Abstract Concept is embodied in the use of Line. If we are impressed with the feeling of Space in a drawing, or Form, then these are its Abstract Concepts.

An expressive and interesting Line can be the main motivation and Visual Idea of a drawing, regardless of the subject matter. It is a raw material available to everyone, but the way it is used will always be of a personal nature because no two people draw alike or respond similarly to a given situation. The same applies to all Abstract Concepts in that each has the potential to be the Visual Idea which the artist can use to personal ends. There are few great artists because there are few who have really understood the value and importance of having a central Idea or Abstract Concept in their work. Furthermore, these few were not diverted in the pursuit of their Ideas by a particular subject matter, philosophy, or criticism.

To simply 'draw a tree' is not in itself a Visual Idea unless great significance is attached to that particular tree. The drawing must display something special which allows it to stand as a meaningful image beyond its Literal Meaning, being the tree. Some feeling or input from the artist must be evident, and the viewer must be guided towards that aspect of the drawing. A work can be visually enticing, or dull and lifeless, and the difference will lie in whether or not it has an energy of its own.

The activity involved in doing the drawing is important, but the resulting image must convey the Idea which the artist intended as a personal Visual statement. Ideas are personal motivations to create something meaningful which can ultimately be shared with others, but this will only be successful if the drawing is clearly understood. Abstract Concepts provide the means to accomplish this.

Colleen Machan

The ability to draw and express Visual Ideas cannot be developed by attempting to 'copy' Nature, varied and full of wonderment though it may be. The artist must learn from Nature, and create works which will inspire similar contemplation and feelings. One does not have to 'learn to draw first', because exploring the potential of the various Abstract Concepts IS learning to draw. They must be used from the beginning to discover one's own preferences and to become aware of the many avenues of Visual Expression available to every artist. Abstract Concepts are not techniques or steps in 'how to draw'. Instead they present a structure for the practice and enjoyment of drawing as a whole. Control over the means of Expression is the goal, but this must be preceded by an awareness of these means.

The dream of Non-Objective Art was to deal with the principles of aesthetics, or Abstract Concepts, as pure elements. Traditional subject matter was considered a distraction from what the artist was 'trying to say' about Line, Shape, Texture, etc., as expressive individual items in a work of Art. Many artists continue to demonstrate that non-objective images are capable of provoking emotional reactions and be visually inspiring. Controversy will always accompany seemingly divergent views of what Art is meant to be, but the underlying essence of a work will always be those elements about it which activate the interest of our eyes, namely the Abstract Concepts.

An investigation of the work of favourite artists is important in order to observe how Abstract Concepts have been used by others. It will be noticed that a dominant Idea is usually evident. In the work of Modigliani, for example, Shapes are given a major role, with Form kept to a subtle level so as not to present a distraction. Matisse is also an artist who has made extensive use of Shapes, often cutting them from paper, while Picasso did many works which dealt with Form as the Visual Idea. Cezanne, Wyeth, Whistler, Rothko, Vasarely, Picasso, Pratt, York Wilson and others have used Composition Ideas to provide a firm structure to their work, and we can learn from them. To look only at the subject matter would be to miss the true Visual Meaning and essence of what the artist is communicating. One must come to realize that meaningful works of Art do not just happen by chance, but are thought out and developed by the artist with a particular goal in mind for each individual piece.

Elements such as Composition, Form, Texture, or the effects produced by the materials used in the drawing, must be in the artist's control. We have no trouble understanding that the subject is at the mercy of the artist, and cannot dictate how a drawing is to be done, but if the artist feels like a slave to the subject and therefore not in control of the situation, the whole question of motivation and creativity will be affected.

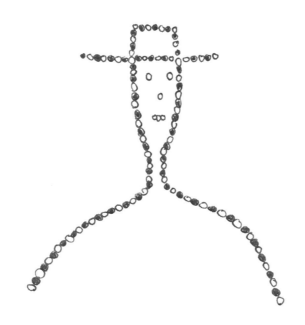

Abstract Concepts provide the means for the artist to take control of the Visual Meaning in a work of Art. They are the 'raw materials' which are available to everyone, but the artist must supply the Visual Ideas and understand that a drawing is expected to be alive and meaningful. The importance which the drawing holds for the person creating it will be transferred to others when it is conceived in a clear and unambiguous manner. This is where the Abstract Concepts come in.

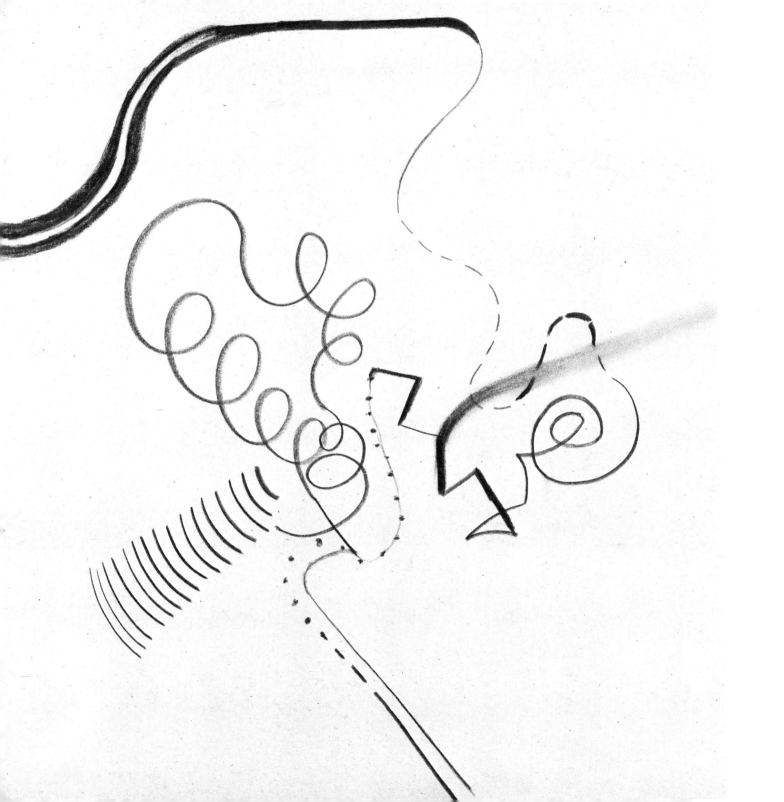

Michelle Orser

6

Chapter One

LINES
as an Abstract Concept

Lines can be used in a drawing for their ability to be appreciated beyond a usefulness in depicting some object or defining a Shape. To give importance to this unique aspect is to employ Lines as an Abstract Concept.

Lines can be black, white, straight, curved, jagged, flowing, or countless other variations which have particular 'personalities'. The potential which exists for them to be visually meaningful, independant of a functional role, is boundless, and requires only the effort on the part of the artist to make use of that fact.

The most mundane use of Lines in drawing is sketching out an Idea or outlining a Shape to determine its general proportions or other characteristics. This is useful in its own way, but may not seem as exciting as being involved with Lines for the interest which they can provide themselves.

Being such a familiar item, often Lines are not taken seriously or given their 'due respect'. When we write a letter the message is usually conveyed in an adequate manner. However when a person takes care to write beautifully and considers the general appearance of the message as a whole, the intrinsic meaning of the letter takes on a different quality. The aesthetic nature of the writing provides a Visual pleasure which cannot be described in words. We also instinctively admire the effort put towards making the writing attractive, assuming also that the person who wrote it enjoyed the involvement of creating a message interesting to look at while conveying a Literal Meaning. The 'appearance' of the writing is its Visual Meaning.

It has been argued that there are no Lines in Nature. This may or may not be considered true, but the fact is that there are Lines in Art. Like Music, Art is not confined to properties which exist in Nature, but has many ingredients which are unique to itself.

Every kind of Line has its own special virtue which must be appreciated as a basic starting point. A straight Line is different from a curve, and a jagged, irregular one presents a different feeling from a smoothly flowing Line. A Line which had been drawn very quickly will convey an energy not to be mistaken for a slow, tediously drawn outline. The very quickness of the Line is its virtue and does not necessarily mean that the artist was simply in a hurry at the time. It is not possible to convey the same kind of energy in a slow, tedious manner. The artist must be in control of the nature of the impression he or she wishes to communicate to others.

Project Number One
Draw as many different kinds of Lines as you are able to think of and create. Continue with this until you honestly can feel the differences among them and can appreciate their individual qualities. Do not attempt to depict objects at this point.

Project Number Two
Draw several objects or non-objective Ideas with identifiable differences in the nature of the Lines used. The dominant interest in the drawings must be the quality and character in the Lines, not the identity of the objects.

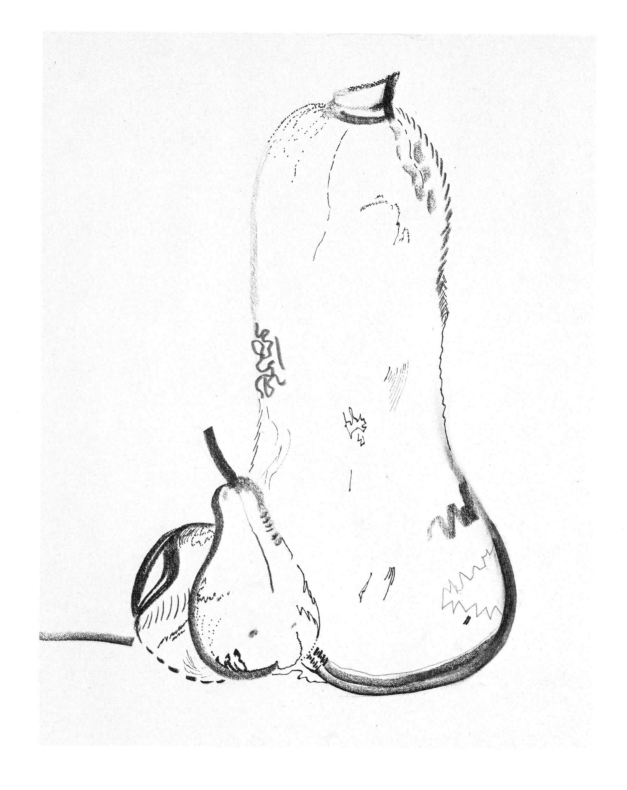

Colleen Machan

9

Sharon Webster

Christie Macmillan

Each tool which is used for drawing has its own qualities and limitations, and therefore one should experiment with a great variety of materials to learn about their potential uses for Visual Expression. Pen and ink can provide a range of tone from black to white. Conte and charcoal are also able to do things which other materials cannot do. Even a sharpened stick dipped in ink will give a Line unlike any other. One comes to realize that through the centuries many items have been used to draw with, and to draw on. The regular Line provided by the newer felt-tipped pens might be scoffed at by Rembrandt if he were here, but he would no doubt have also used them to great advantage. As in all things, the materials are but a starting point, and it is the use which is made of them which is the final test. Nonetheless, the choice of materials does play an important role in the overall impression which the artist must always consider, in relation to a desired quality in the work.

The importance of Lines in Art cannot be over-emphasized, and one should seek out drawings by Rembrandt, Klee, Picasso and David Milne to observe critically the use which they made of Lines in their work. Look at the work of many artists from the past and present, including drawings in magazines, newspapers, etc., to become more fully aware of the real potential and truth in the statement that a Line CAN be interesting.

A 'Line Drawing' must be seen to be just that, and not a mixture of Form, Texture, and other elements all in the one drawing. It will be a recurrent theme in this book that the various Abstract Concepts be considered as separate entities if they are to realize their potentially expressive nature. Occasionally there may be cause to combine them, but one Concept must be the dominant theme in the work if the drawing is to be clearly understood, without conflicting Ideas.

Lines represent a basic 'raw material' for personal Expression, and it is necessary to think in these terms until they become a solid part of one's 'vocabulary'. Only then will come the realization of how fascinating and endless the possibilities are.

11

Dark Lines on light paper will, by nature of the great contrast with the working surface, attract our attention over Lines which are drawn very softly. Thus a dark Line can be used to attract attention to a certain part of the drawing which the artist perhaps wishes to emphasize. A model will darken the area near her eyes to attract attention there, but will not darken the tip of her nose. The artist must also make decisions as to where the attracting areas of the drawing should be. It is not necessarily a case of one section being more important than another, but rather that some direction and focus is required. The model would look like a clown if all parts of her face were attracting in a forceful manner, and so it is with drawing. Everything cannot be a prime interest in a drawing, but at least something should be attracting notice.

Project Number Three
Do a drawing in which the eye (of the viewer) is clearly drawn to some section of it. This will be by using a very dark Line, while other Lines in the drawing are very light.

This is important not only for attracting attention to a certain area, but for breaking up what might otherwise be a drawing of a general nature, with no variations or other features which add special interest.

Monica Shelton

Micheline Pharand

14

The virtue of a Line can be in its regularity and sense of sureness as it moves about on the page without seeming to have either a beginning or an end. This approach suits a pen very well, and requires confidence on the part of the artist. This is but one 'game' which can be played with Lines. Another might be drawing intentionally with an erratic, nervous Line, or creating a Line with the use of a series of dots or x's. Drawing while looking only at the subject and not at the paper is useful in sharpening the communication between one's eye and hand, placing a stronger emphasis than usual on the sense of observation. However, the real test of a Line is how we see it in the drawing, rather than how it may have gotten there.

Project Number Four

Do a large drawing using a minimum number of Lines which flow in a steady manner throughout the drawing. There should be no Lines seeming to end in 'mid air', which will involve carrying them to the perimeter of the paper where necessary.

Lines which display some character are not only important for the sake of adding interest to the drawing, but also because they contribute their own vitality and meaning. The virtue of a quickly drawn Line is its very quickness, regardless of the medium with which it is drawn or the particular subject matter. Its energy comes through to the viewer even years after the original stroke. A timid Line will convey a mood of hesitancy, and a Line drawn with real sensitivity towards the subject will be appreciated as such.

Lines can have 'feelings' such as horizontal, vertical, rhythmic, heavy or light, and it is in this manner that they express their personalities. The artist must be conscious of this when working on a drawing and the viewer should be sensitive to these feelings as well in order to derive a better understanding of the work itself. To view Lines as static and lifeless items which serve only a funtional role will be missing out on one of the basic means of appreciation in Art. A Line may tell us something about the subject, but it will also be telling us about itself. Paul Klee, Picasso, and David Hockney are noted for their ability to instill life into Lines.

Project Number Five

Do a series of drawings employing Lines which would appear to have feelings of some kind. This could include 'feeling long' or 'feeling nervous' etc.

Allison Fraser

17

There are many things in Nature which have a Linear quality as we think of tall grass, strands of hair, or grains of wood etc. Our own identity can be recorded by the uniqueness of the Lines which make up our fingerprints, and palm-readers find a great deal of interest in the Lines on our hands. Old age creates Lines on faces and sunlight streaming through clouds creates Lines which have a dramatic effect. Each kind of Line has its own character as it is also observed that occasionally a Line is light on a dark background or dark on a light ground. Everything about a Line, including its environment, affects the quality of it in some way. The argument concerning Lines in Nature relates to the fact that even a strand of hair has 'body', but of interest to the artist is the essence of its Linear quality. As with all things, much can be learned from observations of Nature. However, Nature is not there to be 'copied', but to be inspiring.

Project Number Six

Drawing from Nature, emphasize the Linear quality of the things which you see. Give attention to their character and uniqueness. Observe the relationships they have with their environment, especially regarding tonal considerations.

Allison Husband

19

A vital element in drawing is that of personal discovery, as only experimenting and 'being brave' will reveal. Often a person will experiment freely with non-objective Ideas, then unfortunately revert to using ordinary Lines when drawing an object or figure. It seems as though interesting Lines are only considered when there is no subject-matter to 'fall back on'. Simply because an object is 'recognizable' does not necessarily make it interesting to look at.

'Thinking about Lines' and seeking them out in the works of others to be further aware of their potential in drawing is essential. Using them in a positive manner as a regular and defined approach to a drawing will provide a person with a skill and control over the Expression which Lines are able to display.

Lines, however made and for whatever purpose, are a basic tool for the artist. They may be crisp and clean, or smudged and vague, but their presence can be felt as a meaningful Expression in their own right. Lines can attract attention and titillate the sense of sight, and therefore must be considered a major factor in the study and appreciation of drawing.

Conyers Barker

Eve Benelow

Kathy Hoffman

26

Chapter Two

SHAPES
as an Abstract Concept

By definition a Shape is two-dimensional or flat in character. It may be depicted with the use of Lines, but will be recognized as being what the artist wishes the viewer to be aware of when looking at the work. The Lines are employed functionally and we are conscious of the Shape rather than the Lines which create it.

Cut-outs with paper are Shapes, and we would have little trouble perceiving leaves or footprints in the same way. However, we might have difficulty in thinking of a horse as a Shape. This is clearly because we consider it in terms of bulk and weight, but if we were to view it as a silhouette, we might be surprised at how interesting a Shape it possesses.

Everything has a Shape. The Pyramids, clouds, a leg, a bird, a sculpture, or Michael Snow's 'Walking Woman', are all contained in Shapes which have only to be observed and appreciated. As it is with Lines, Shapes can be very different from each other and possess individual qualities. Many things can be readily identified by their Shapes and some may appear to us as being very beautiful, while others seem to be quite ordinary or non-descript. As a Visual phenomenon, Shapes play a major role in Art.

Since drawing deals with a two-dimensional activity, it is essential to appreciate the potential of the silhouette, or Shape of things to be interesting, expressive, and meaningful. We have to accept the fact that the drawing surface is flat, and go on to make the best use of it.

The outer edge of a Shape is often referred to as its 'Line'. A potter shaping a bowl will observe it from the side to determine whether or not it has 'good Lines', meaning an agreeable Shape. Also a fashion designer will want an article of clothing to have 'good Lines'. In this respect there is common ground between Lines and Shapes.

Project Number Seven

Draw the silhouetted Shapes of several items, making an effort to be as accurate as possible in your observations and renderings of them. This careful approach will increase the appreciation of their Shapes.

Shapes in Nature are generally quite different from those which are man-made. A sense of growth and movement is present in Natural Shapes, while those which are man-made tend to be more geometric and static. However, we are familiar with both in our daily experiences. Some are more agreeable than others, but each has its own character which we respond to.

Project Number Eight

Draw many kinds of non-objective Shapes. The edges should be well-defined, and some attempt should be made to give them character, or a 'personality' of their own.

Project Number Nine

Draw a border along the edge of the drawing surface, which would define the rectangle which will be 'dealt with'. Divide this area into several sections, and think of them as Shapes. Be conscious of the amount of area they occupy in relation to each other. This should be repeated several times using various numbers of Shapes, and various sizes and relationships.

Project Number Ten

As in the previous project, draw in a defined perimeter. Using still-life objects, draw in their Shapes, remaining conscious of the amount of area they have in relation to each other, and in relation to the overall area of the drawing. These Shapes should be 'allowed' to overlap to create a feeling of transparency and maintain a sense of flatness.

James Taylor

30

A Negative area is understood to be that part of the drawing which does not represent the actual subject (which is considered the Positive area) but which surrounds and in a way is displaced by it. Appreciation of Positive and Negative relationships is a very important aspect of drawing because wherever there is one, the other will be present also. Although we are generally more attracted to the Positive elements, both are important to the total effect of the drawing, and must be considered by the artist.

A small Shape on a large surface will have a different impact than a large Shape which allows the Negative area less opportunity to dominate the page. Somewhere there is always a comfortable balance in Visual terms in which each acts to enhance the other.

Project Number Eleven

From a model, draw the overall Shape or silhouette using a continuous Line to define the edge. Be conscious of the Positive and Negative elements of the whole drawing, including their respective Shapes, and the areas which they occupy.

Project Number Twelve

Do a drawing from a model in which the Shape is developed as a mass growing out from the centre. No attempt should be made to suggest Form, as this would detract from an appreciation of the Shape.

Project Number Thirteen

Do a drawing from a model in which all elements are seen as Shapes, and rendered accordingly in a well-defined manner. Some will be darker than others, and have other individual characteristics such as the Shape and tone of the hair, hands, folds in the clothing, etc. They will form a unified whole because they all combine to become the overall Shape of the figure.

Janis Gadowski

33   Mark Gillham

A Shape serves a functional purpose when used to represent or suggest a familiar subject. Its aesthetic aspect involves its own Visual quality apart from the fact of it being accurate or not to the subject which it is representing. It may be flowing, angular or have any other quality which makes it visually interesting to the viewer. Modigliani dealt largely with an appreciation of Shapes, and manipulated and distorted them until he was satisfied with the harmony and general feeling which he was attempting to achieve in the whole Composition. The figures are still 'figures', but it is the quality of the Shapes which gives the work its Visual Meaning. Form is kept to a very subtle level in order not to detract from the central idea of the Shapes. As with other Abstract Concepts, Shapes cannot be seen and appreciated if other elements are also attracting attention.

When the artist has made it clear what the drawing is concerned with, we can comfortably relate to that Idea, regardless of what the subject may be. Naturally we like to know what we are supposed to be looking at, and if the artist has not made that clear, it is possible that he has not made a decision about it himself. When the Idea is apparent, we feel that the artist is in control, and we are able to relax and enjoy the drawing for what it is meant to be. If we don't happen to like the drawing, at least we know what it is that we aren't liking, in this instance, the Shapes.

Simplifying situations in order to clarify an Idea is an important factor in drawing. If we direct our thoughts to a specific aspect of something such as a tree or a figure, rather than try to take in everything at once, we see it more clearly, and as a result will draw that Idea more clearly. We can get involved with the Shape without concern for all its other aspects only when we specifically deal with the Shape.

Areas of shadow, especially those which occur when there is a strong light on the subject, can also be considered in terms of their Shapes. Because they are always changing, they take on no regular or familiar configurations, but rather are unique, sometimes with unusual and unexpected dimensions. As mentioned above, they require LOOKING FOR and defining in a positive way in the drawing.

Project Number Fourteen
Do a drawing in which the shadow areas are bravely sought out in the subject, and bravely defined. Their areas should be toned in a direct manner, so that it is clearly understood that the Shapes are the concern, and not the Line which contains them.

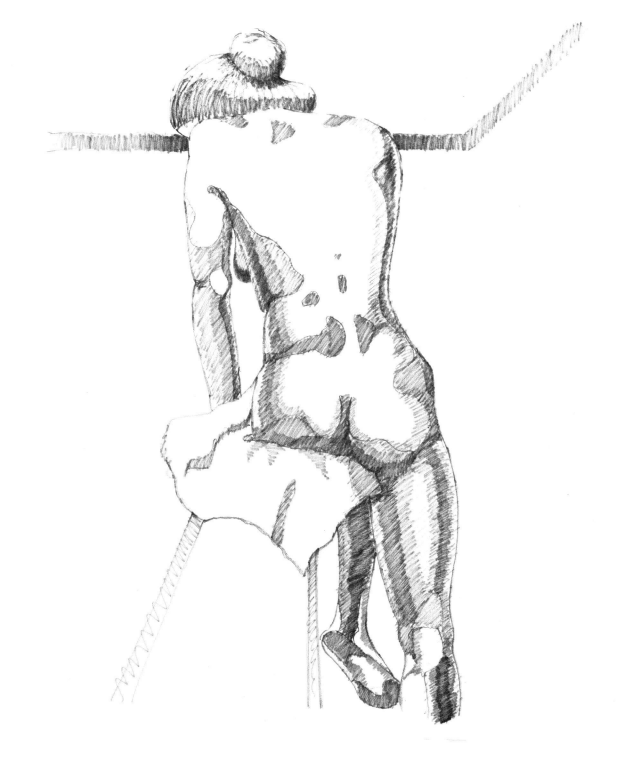

Gary Owen

35

Van Gogh used Shapes to contain his Ideas about Colour, often using outlines to clearly define them. Many works by Paul Klee are 'about Shapes', while other are 'about Lines'. In the work of Andrew Wyeth or Greg Curnoe we are aware of the Shapes of things as a strong feature in the Compositions. Picasso was free with his distortions of Shapes to his own ends, and we should also be appreciative of the flowing Shapes in East Indian miniatures and Japanese woodcuts.

Shapes and Lines are very different, and this difference is immediately apparent when they are seen together in a drawing. As a result they can be used together to provide contrast and to complement each other.

Shapes have a role in Art far greater than simply depicting some familiar item. The use of Shapes in a symbolic manner, such as a 'heart' or an arrow etc., makes them familiar to us in this functional way also, but their ability to be energetic and visually meaningful to a point where they can be admired 'for their Shape' is the essence of what a Shape can be.

Barry Shelton

Barbara Robillard

Chapter Three

FORM
as an Abstract Concept

Form refers to the suggestion in a drawing of an object's third dimension, or fullness. Form is therefore fundamentally different from Shape which deals solely with flat, two-dimensional qualities. We are familiar with the fullness of things in Nature, and to want to suggest this aspect in a drawing seems a natural thing in many cases. When we see Form in a work of Art we relate comfortably to it, and have a sense of being further informed about the subject. That is its functional role.

Dealing with the illusion or depiction of Form as a prime concern in a drawing, beyond simply its functional aspect, can provide its own special Visual Meaning. In other words, Form can be very interesting in itself, regardless of the particular subject matter, and is capable of being the dominant interest, or Visual Idea, in a work. Form provides 'body' and enlightens the viewer about the fullness of things, but it can also be so fascinating that we may not be aware of the Shape nor be overly concerned about the subject matter.

There are endless approaches to Form, but the main ingredient is the artist's intent for it to be a feature in the work. Where function ends, aesthetics or Visual fascination begins.

Monica Shelton

41

Barry Shelton

42

Form Study Number One

A Single Light Source

The quality of light can affect the general mood and influence the appearance of things. For example, a darkened room with a single candle burning in the centre of the table which is set for a meal and around which people are sitting, will focus the attention on the areas receiving light, with the shadow areas seeming to fade into the darkness of the room. The mood seems peaceful and poetic, with everything including the food, looking good. As soon as overhead electric lights are turned on the mood vanishes!

Also how clean and fresh everything looks in the morning when sunlight comes streaming into the room! How round and full the fruit on the table looks and how good the whole situation makes us feel! Later on in the day as the light becomes more general we tend to forget how wholesome things had appeared that morning, and how good it made us feel.

We respond favourably to similarly controlled situations in a drawing, but the artist is not always in charge of the quality of light in the immediate environment. It is often necessary, therefore, to establish an arbitrary light source for the drawing in order to organize the light and dark areas and develop a feeling of Form. Moods of tranquility or vibrant feelings of strong sunlight can be achieved simply by the artist's declaration of that intention. The ability to establish arbitrary situations for a drawing is an important aspect of creativity.

The fullness of an object is clearest when there is a light shining onto it from a single source, rather than several lights from many directions as is often the case in reality. A single light creates an orderly impression of light and dark (shadow) areas which emphasizes the Form as well as presenting a drawing which has an interesting pattern of light and dark areas.

Under a strong light details on the surface of a subject become diffuse, and shadows obscure those details on the opposite side, and we are thus made aware of the Form over other interests such as surface patterns or Textures. The awareness of Form, in relation to surface features, or Shape, is affected by the strength of the light.

Drawing onto the Negative areas of the paper will provide contrast, and allow the light areas of the object to be appreciated. The greater this contrast is, the greater will appear the quality of the light on the object. In this manner, dark sections of the drawing serve two basic roles; to suggest the shadow areas of the object, and to make one more aware of the light areas by providing a contrasting tone on the Negative side of it.

As with most cases which appear 'too simple', this approach requires concentration and an understanding of the importance of consistency. The works of Vermeer, Seurat, and LeMoine Fitzgerald, to name only three artists who have employed this approach to advantage, do not appear to be overly simple. The gentle use of Form in many early Chinese scrolls should also be made familiar. Holding onto a basically simple Idea throughout a drawing very often proves to be the most difficult, but in the end the most rewarding part of it.

Since Lines and Shapes refer to two-dimensional aspects, their evidence in a drawing which deals with Form, should be kept to a minimum, or not be apparent at all. Lines which may have been used to define the Shape which contains the Form, should become 'lost' in the process of developing the drawing.

Project Number Fifteen

Draw a leg or other rounded item in as simple terms as possible while defining its Shape. Establish an arbitrary light direction and develop the areas of light and dark in a manner sensitive to the Form of the subject, and make use of the Negative areas of the page to provide contrast to the light parts of the subject. Drawing on the Negative area adjoining the shadow areas of the subject will serve to 'quieten' the whole area so that the main interest will be on the light areas of the drawing. No Lines should be in evidence in the finished work.

Project Number Sixteen

Develop a major drawing using still-life, a figure, or a non-objective approach, in which an arbitrary source of light is employed. Negative areas should be considered important and developed accordingly, and it should be clear to any viewer that 'light and Form' is the central Idea of the drawing.

Project Number Seventeen
Having established an assumed light source as in the previous projects, develop a drawing using only Line as a technique. Heavy or dark Lines will be used to suggest the shadowed sides, with soft and light Lines to suggest those areas facing the light source. As with other Ideas, consistency with the approach is the important and perhaps most difficult aspect.

Form Study Number Two

Planes

A 'plane' is understood to have a flat surface, such as the side of a box, and is normally seen to have a single or uniform tonal quality. The angle of the plane in relation to the source of light determines its tone, and therefore the more it turns away from the light source, the darker it will be.

It is easy to appreciate the sides of a box as 'planes', but it would seem that an apple does not have similar features because it is round in character. Its essence is one of fullness and body rather than of flatness. Nonetheless we are aware that it has a top, bottom, left and right sides and a front and back when viewed under various lighting conditions. A direct light from above will clearly separate the top from the bottom because one will be 'generally light' and the other 'generally dark'. If the light were to shine from either side, the same situation will occur with the side 'planes'. When an area seems to have a general tonal quality it can be thought of as being a plane, and appreciated as such.

The human body, or other objects more complex than an apple, also have general areas which face in one direction or another, and these planes can be simplified and analysed in an arbitrary way, or with the help of controlled lighting on the subject. To simplify curved areas into planes and angles does not necessarily destroy their character, but gives them a new character and a solid structure, bringing out a clear three-dimensional understanding.

It will be observed that in a drawing which is conceived in terms of planes and delineated with straight Lines rather than curves, a certain harmony exists through the consistent nature of the approach.

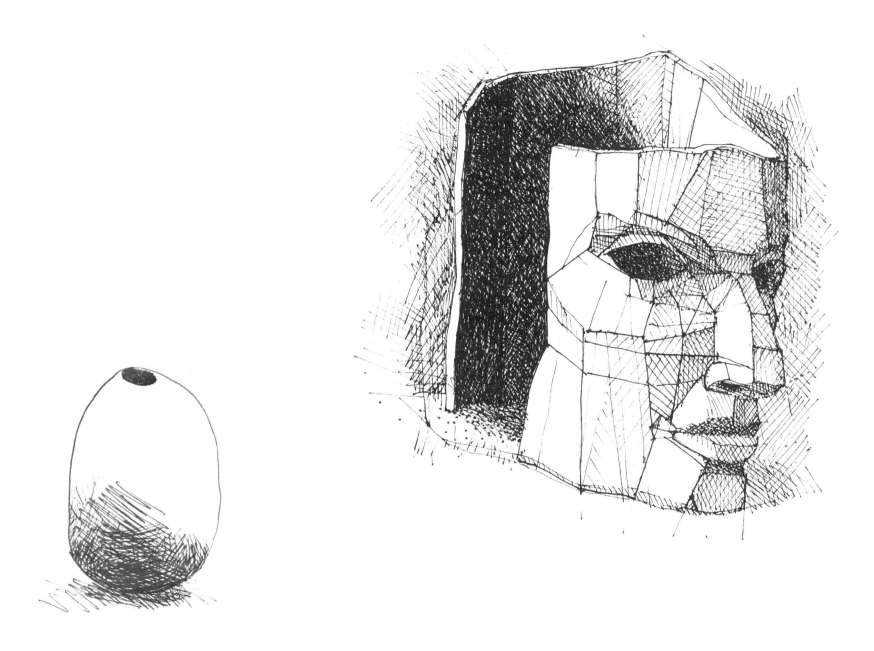

47

Project Number Eighteen
Simplify rounded objects into planes, which may be conceived as
Line, or Form drawings using tones for areas of light and shade.
Continue with several real or imaginary objects to establish a con-
scious awareness of angles and directions in which various sec-
tions or planes face.

49

Rolf Eckhardt

50

Form Study Number Three

Foreshortening

The apparent shortening of the distance between elements when they are viewed from an oblique angle, and the seeming distortion which occurs in the relative sizes and Shapes of them, is a Visual phenomenon the artist is often obliged to consider. The chief difficulty when drawing such a setting is that of observation and 'believing our eyes' rather than proceeding, armed with the knowledge of what the real proportions and Shapes are like.

If an artist wishes to draw a group of apples which are scattered about on a table, he or she will not likely take out a ruler and start measuring actual distances between them, and their sizes etc. Instead one will observe the situation as it appears to be from the particular place it is viewed from. The spaces between the apples will appear shorter than is known to be the case, and the nearer ones will seem larger than those farther away. Details concerning the nearest will be more apparent and they will seem to be more important generally.

The same situation occurs when a figure or any other object is viewed from an extreme position and individual parts seem to become distorted. The familiar example of someone with a hand outstretched towards the viewer, appearing to protrude right out of the drawing, shows the effects of foreshortening being used to emphasize a particular Idea.

Project Number Nineteen
Spread a group of similar sized objects around on a table and after observing them for a time, do a drawing which will clearly demonstrate their positions in Space.

Project Number Twenty

a. *Draw a reclining figure from an extreme angle. Observe the relative sizes and Shapes of the various parts of the body, making note of apparent distortions which seem to occur. Observe the proportions and Shapes as you see them, rather than as you know them to be.*

b. *Repeat the same Idea, viewing the figure from the opposite angle.*

c. *Draw the same reclining figure from a position directly in front.*

Project Number Twenty-one

Draw a seated figure from a casual angle. Exaggerate the nearest parts to emphasize the foreshortening aspect in the drawing. One arm will be nearer than the other and as a result will be drawn clearly larger so that there will visually be no doubt about its position.

Form Study Number Four

Attractions

A loud noise on an otherwise quiet afternoon will immediately be noticed, and a dark Line or area on an otherwise light drawing will also be noticed at first glance, appearing nearer as a result. Therefore a dark section on a drawing can be used to advantage to help emphasize the closeness of something in relation to other elements.

The location in Space of the parts of a subject is important when the Idea is to provide a feeling of fullness. A large ball, for example, will have its front centre section much closer to the viewer than the sides which are curving away. Visually this is not always clearly apparent, but our knowledge of the ball sustains us. However the artist must clarify the situation in a drawing by being sensitive to the nearness of the closer sections. This can be achieved by a controlled use of the darks in the drawing to represent the nearest parts of the object.

In this approach the actual tones and patterns on the object are not to be considered, rather the position in relation to the artist is the central concern. A part of it may be darker than another area in actuality, but if other sections are nearer to the artist, the 'dark sections' must be rendered light. The proximity in Space is the only criterion regarding the tonal value given to particular items. This phenomenon occurs in Nature and the paleness of distant hills is a familiar sight. A foggy morning serves to emphasize this idea even more.

When only a few inches are involved such as when drawing a head, the tonal changes are not so apparent and the artist must be very sensitive to relative positions, and sometimes exaggerate the effects so that the drawing will not appear flat, and thus contrary to the intended sense of Form.

When the general tone of a drawing is dark, light sections can be used to suggest close-ness, with values gradually deepening as they recede into the background. Whether the darks or the lights advance in a drawing is a decision made by the artist, and the situation presented will be one of order that can be easily related to and understood.

Project Number Twenty-two

a. *Do a drawing of any subject in which the darks are clearly the nearer parts, with tones graduating back to the white of the paper. The location in Space should be the only determining factor regarding lights and darks.*

b. *Do a Line drawing based on the above Idea.*

Project Number Twenty-three

Do a drawing in which all elements deepen in tone as they recede. The furthest sections, being those in the area understood to be in the background, will develop to black, with the nearest points remaining the white of the paper.

'Detail' in a drawing can serve the same function as tonal values to emphasize the Form of an object. As sections recede, such as decoration around the side of a vase, or article of clothing, they can receive less attention from the artist during the execution of the drawing which would allow them to 'settle back' and take their place in relation to other parts of the subject. The artist has but to emphasize the diffusion of detail in a drawing for the Form Idea to be clearly understood. Areas of well-defined detail will appear 'close', because they will be attracting the eye.

Project Number Twenty-four

Do a drawing of any subject, whether real or imaginary, in which a greater amount of attention is given to the assumed nearer sections. The more distant parts will appear casual and hence not attract immediate notice.

Barry Shelton

55

Form Study Number Five
Edges

The nature of the edges of things depicted in a drawing which has its central focus on Form is always important. A clearly defined edge is valuable when the concern is with Shapes, but is an unwanted element when the interest is with Form and where a defined edge will merely 'flatten' the Idea.

An edge represents the outer boundary of an object, or occurs when planes meet and change direction, such as the adjoining sides of a box. If these edges are drawn soft and elusive, the Idea concerning the essence of the box will be confused. On the other hand, if the edges of a ball were drawn sharply this also would be contradictory to the Idea of the ball, and relate more to a flat circle. A vase or other cylindrical object has edges which slowly turn away from us regardless at which angle we view it from, and therefore must appear elusive in a drawing if it is not to seem to be depicting a flat Shape. A Form is contained within a Shape, but the kind of edge used in the drawing will largely determine how we understand the intentions of the artist regarding Shape or Form.

The indistinguishable nature of the edge between light and dark sides of a round object creates an impression of its Form, but the quality of the outer edge where it meets with the Negative area is also important. If this outer edge contrasts greatly with the adjoining section of the drawing, it will attract attention to itself. To avoid this unwanted situation, the contrasts should be in accordance with the artist's Idea about light and Form, and the edges themselves should be soft and vague rather than clear and crisp.

Softening the edges, increasing or reducing contrasts, and being generally sensitive to the nature of the edges in a drawing is not difficult to do, but does require the artist's concern. The situation as we understand it in the drawing must be the central issue, rather than how things might appear in reality. Awareness of the quality of edges as they appear in Nature will help make one more sensitive and consciously in control of the edges in drawing. Concern about Form in a drawing must necessarily be accompanied by attention to the edges, their relationship to the essence of the subject, and to the quality of the drawing as a whole.

Project Number Twenty-five
Do a drawing of real or imaginary Ideas in which particular attention is paid to the quality of the edges of everything in the drawing. No edge should be carelessly drawn, or left unconsidered.

Form Study Number Six

Sculpture

A great deal can be learned about the suggestion of the third dimension by observing the drawings of sculptors, such as those of Henry Moore, for example. Picasso also did very sculptural drawings as part of his continual experimenting with Visual Ideas, and Form in particular.

The attention is focussed on developing a solid feeling of structure in the subject which seems to be in the open air, rather than on a flat drawing surface. Anything which can add to the sense of Form, such as Lines following the contour of the object, or strong Lines which feel like stone, contribute to the overall sense of fullness. Any 'wooliness' in the drawing will therefore weaken the intended impression. Even the sheep drawings by Moore present solid, rather than soft animals, and Picasso's figures often seem to be carved in stone.

Atmospheric conditions cause the Form of things in Nature to be unclear, but when the artist wishes the drawing to be crisp and the Form to be clearly apparent and 'sculptural', that artist has only to insist on it and enforce the intention onto the drawing. Creativity is developing an Idea and using one's imagination towards realizing it in Visual terms.

Project Number Twenty-six

Do a drawing of real or imaginary subjects in which the intention is to imbue them with a solid feeling as though they were carved from wood or made of clay. A firm hand is required, and a resolve to have the drawing feel somehow free of the page.

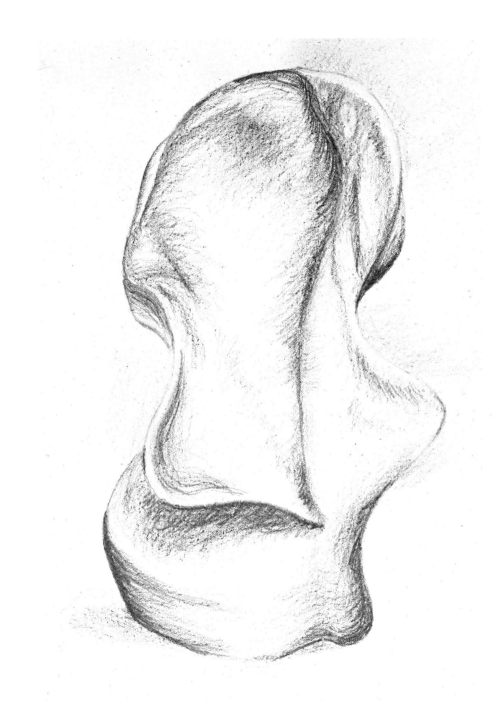

Kelley Penhale

59

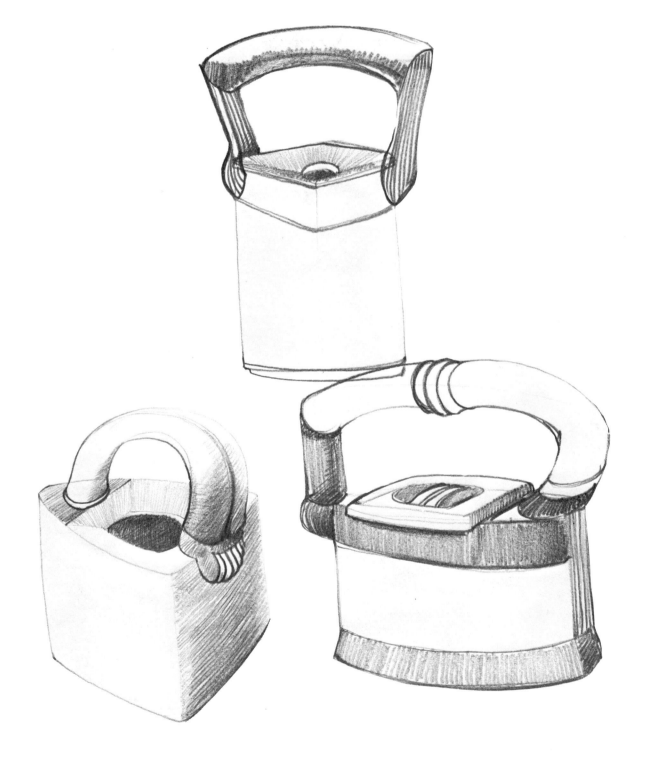

Cindy Struik

61

Tracey Martin

62

63

Mary Lou Jones

65

Chapter Four

TEXTURE
as an Abstract Concept

Everything in Nature has a surface quality apart from its Colour and Shape. This is its Texture. We are familiar with the surfaces of apples and oranges, and take their difference for granted. Similarly we would not likely confuse silk with burlap even if they were the same Colour. Snow in winter has a surface quality different from that of the lawn in summer, and it seems that no two things are alike, visually or physically. Nature is infinitely varied in all of its many aspects.

In drawing we have only the sense of sight to deal with, and our eyes must be the sensitive part of us. We respond to the surface quality in a drawing for the interest which it provides visually, aside from possibly identifying a familiar item. Any character which an area displays can be a meaningful addition to a drawing.

The nature of the paper's surface will affect the impression we get of the drawing, but any quality other than that must be put there by the artist. There are many ways to create interest in a drawing apart from using Lines, Shapes, Form, etc., or the use of tone to provide contrasts. An area may be light or dark, and this effect can be achieved by a Texture such as a series of parallel Lines, for example, or many small marks on the page, which will make the area more interesting than if it was simply toned in a general way. As well as providing the necessary tonal quality, the surface will also be visually alive and therefore 'meaningful'.

The true nature of a Texture is that it presents an overall, general quality. This allows the entire surface to be appreciated as a unit but does not mean that it is free of irregularities. Textures may be very accidental or casual in manner, or very ordered and geometric. They may also be very 'quiet' and subtle, or 'noisy' and energetic.

Project Number Twenty-seven

Experiment with several different KINDS of Textures. Do not get involved with depicting Shapes, but deal solely with surface effects to make them interesting. Use various materials such as pen and ink, pencil, conte, fingers, sponge, sticks, or feathers.

Drawing is an Art form generally considered to employ only one Colour, and therefore Textures can play the role of providing Visual enticements for the eye which would otherwise be done with the use of Colour. Even a very subtle Texture can add life to an area intended to remain 'in the background' and a lively Textured area can give 'Colour' to an area intended to attract and hold the attention of the viewer.

Textures can be dense, and therefore dark, or scattered and open, which would 'read' as light. Anything can be used to create Textures in a drawing. It may be small x's, dots, circles, letters, splattered ink, or a combination of effects, including scribbling and cross-hatching. The essential element is the artist's awareness of what they can do for a drawing.

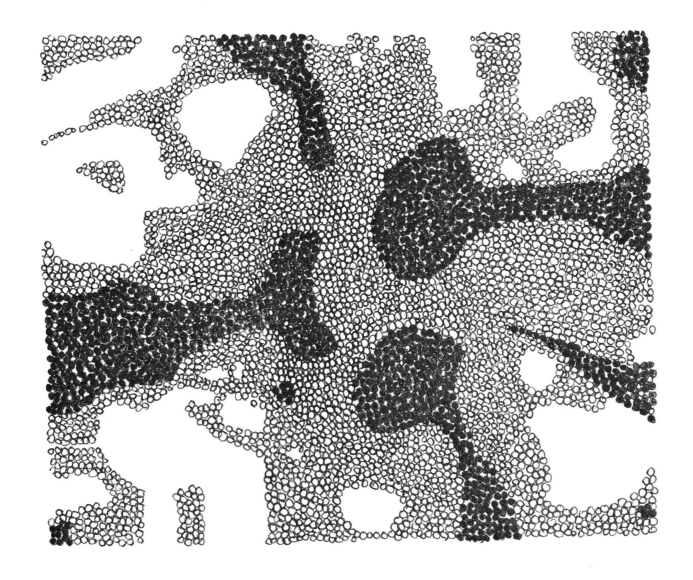

The more attention given to an area by the artist, the more interesting and richer it will be. This was well known by the monks who created the 'Book of Kells' and those who made the valuable Persian carpets. They are beautiful and fascinating because the trouble was taken to make them so. It is not a question of having the time to do it, which is a common argument, but of possessing an awareness of aesthetic possibilities. They knew that their efforts were infinitely worthwhile. Sometimes there is no alternative to patient work when a particular richness is the goal.

An appreciation of the richness of natural Textures is important as a reminder of the intricate and endlessly varied Visual impressions which they present. Old boards, stones, fields, crowds of people, or a hillside covered with trees, have individual qualities. Sometimes we see things as a mass, such as when we look at a tree, and are not necessarily aware of each of its leaves. We know that even each leaf is a unique thing, even as each pen stroke in a Textured area of a drawing is a unique and separate item when regarded as such.

Nature is never dull and always provides some irregularities or patterns within Textured areas to relieve the eyes of the viewer. Shadow areas in a tree, or grains in an old board create a sense of pattern as part of the overall Texture which can also be appreciated as a separate Visual element. On the other hand, a man-made Texture such as sandpaper which is produced for a particular function is not inspiring to look at because it is regular and predictable.

Robert Kemp

Monica Shelton

Gryphon summer season most successful ever

The Gryphon Theatre reports that its summer season has been the most successful in its history.

Attendance for the season's five plays rose to 16,581 this year from last year's total of 14,913. Box office receipts totalled a record $98,497.

Vernon Chapman, Gryphon's artistic director and administrator for the past four years, will return again next year as artistic director.

Chapman's administrative duties will be shared by Margaret Wright, office manager, and Judith French, who joins the Gryphon Theatre to act as comptroller with an emphasis on publicity and fundraising.

While Gryphon Theatre is not producing any shows during the winter months it is sponsoring several performances.

Billy Bishop Goes To War, already sold out, will be presented on November 10 and The Famous People Players will perform on April 3.

Schoolchildren will be treated to an exclusive performance of The Dream Burger Dilemma on November 9. The Railroad show will be presented in the spring.

Bolivians to perform

Los Tawa (The Four), a musical group from Bolivia, will be performing in Barrie on October 13.

The group has won a number of awards in national festivals of folk music in Bolivia, and has been invited to play for two Bolivian presidents. The four musicians have put out two records.

Los Tawa is displaying a variety of unique instruments on a coast-to-coast tour of Canada, performig in the churches of the Baptist Federation of Canada.

The Barrie concert will be held in the First Baptist Church starting at 7:30 p.m. For more information, call 728-5801.

...ma Tordiff of Barrie makes sure
...f her paintings is hung straight.
...ls and watercolors are currently
...at the Barrie Art Club Gallery in
...own Centre. The exhibition is
...d in a series which opened with
...of Bettina Harvie. Tordiff was a
...Harvie's. She told The Banner
...interested in color and likes the
...of painting.

...ent contest
...es accepted

...h school
...e a chance
...0 universi-
...ship for

form of prose. Poetry, however, is not eligible.

Copies of the official rules and regulations

Toy display at children's centre

A homemade toy display and demonstration will be held at the Toy Chest at the Sunny Park Children's Centre in Barrie on Thursday, October 15 between noon and 6 p.m..

On November 19, a session is scheduled on choosing toys that are safe and durable, and a Christmas party will be held on December 17.

The centre is located at 190 Cook St. For more information, call 726-0701.

The printed page of a newspaper presents a Texture, and only when we look closely at it do we begin to read or seek out specific items. Photographs and large type used for headlines present a pattern which breaks up the overall effect of the text, and gives relief to the eyes. This is done intentionally by the designers of the newspaper to make the page more interesting to look at. A sense of organization is also provided in that we aren't confronted with a solid mass of text with no apparent guide or attracting sections.

A lace table-cloth has a special Texture which is broken up visually by the pattern which comprises it. The feeling of the lace is throughout and binds the entire design together. We have, therefore, no trouble in thinking of the table-cloth as a unit.

The design or pattern in the table-cloth, or the grains in an old board remain a part of the whole because they share a quality or essence which binds together the parts in our perception of them. This quality is another function of Texture as it creates a unifying situation. A drawing which is done entirely with short pencil strokes will have a harmony as well because of the unifying nature of the technique employed. It presents itself as an overall Texture because all aspects share a similar Visual effect.

The attention which Van Gogh paid to Textures in his drawings relates with the concern he gave to Colour in his painting. We are also indebted to Seurat for the pointillism or 'dot technique'. This was originally employed for using dots of Colour, but the unifying nature of the Texture and its apparent liveliness makes a valuable addition to anyone's vocabulary of Visual possibilities.

Barrie Banner

A drawing done with a constant technique will have a Texture as a result, but this alone will not make the drawing meaningful in terms of its Texture. The surface quality must be 'special' in some way if it is to attract attention and be involving for the artist in the process.

Textures provide a surface interest which can be rich and 'Colourful'. It serves as a tonal quality when needed, and has the ability to give the drawing an inter-woven and harmonious feeling. The artist must however be conscious of when a Texture is required, and when it could produce a negative effect in a drawing. If a Shape, for example, is very agreeable and well proportioned, the employment of Texture on its surface may detract from our appreciation of the Shape.

As with all Abstract Concepts, Textures have the potential to be an expressive force in a work of Art or to be a subtle addition to the richness of a work which perhaps employs a different Concept as its dominant Idea.

We are surrounded by Textures in Nature, our homes, and our clothes, and they play a dominant role in many instances. All that is required for them to be important assets in a drawing is for the artist to explore their possibilities and to take advantage of them.

Project Number Thirty
Do a drawing with a single Texture Idea such as cross-hatching, or small circles, etc. Vary the intensity and include pattern effects or Form.

Veronica Martin

John Coburn

Linda Kinsey

79

Richard Dunbrook

80

Chapter Five

Space and Perspective

as Abstract Concepts

Perspective deals with the problem of presenting objects as they might appear in Nature, and the principles concerning it may be relied upon to provide a feeling of depth in a drawing. The artist is thus able to consider his drawing in terms of Space, rather than solely as a flat surface.

The understanding of Form, Space, and Perspective, in a drawing relies in part on our knowledge of how things really are in Nature. From a simple suggestion our imagination is able to complete the Idea in our mind, and feel comfortable in doing so.

In our everyday life we are not overly aware of Perspective as a phenomenon because being so familiar with its effects we take them for granted. On seeing a small barn with tiny horses nearby we instinctively know that they are normal in size and are simply a distance away. Similarly when a road appears to be ending in a point, we know that in fact it is as wide there as at any other place. The road appears to become narrow because it is reaching into the distance. When we see similar situations in a drawing we understand them in the same way.

The EYE OF THE ARTIST is the critical item as all things relate to it. When someone looks at a drawing that person is effectively standing in the shoes of the artist, sharing the same Eye Level and looking out to the same Vanishing Point.

The Horizon Line and Eye Level are synonymous. When our Eye Level moves up or down (with our eyes) as it does when we are standing or sitting, so does the Horizon Line. This is most in evidence when we look out over a body of water. Vanishing Points are always on the Horizon Line, and will relate to where we are standing and to our direct Line of Vision, which is the direction in which we are looking. Whether we are looking up, down, or sideways, will naturally determine how we perceive things.

Natural Laws Concerning Perspective

1. Objects appear to diminish in size as they recede. This is in accordance with imaginary straight Lines which relate to the Eye Level (Horizon Line) and the Line of Vision. The spot where objects seem to disappear when taken to their farthest extreme in Space is referred to as the Vanishing Point.

2. Colours, Textures, and Tones, become duller as they recede, and contrasts which appear strong at close range are weak when viewed from a distance.

3. Details and Edges which are sharp and clear become diffused and more difficult to distinguish as they recede from view.

84

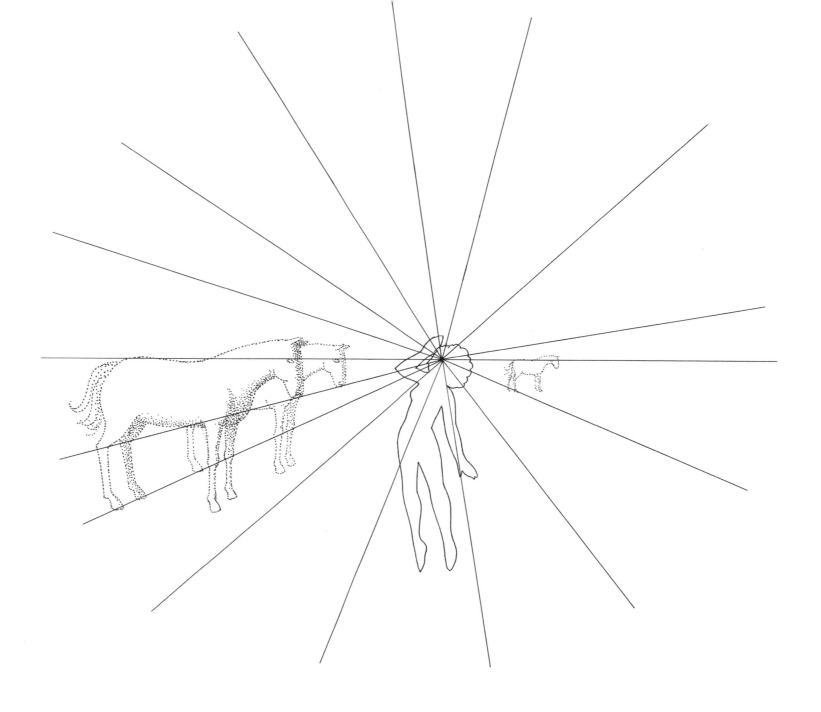

One Point Perspective

This is the most simple form of Perspective and all that is required is to establish an Eye Level (Horizon Line) on the page, and a Vanishing Point on that same Line. A Picture Plane is understood to be a vertical rectangle which represents the artist's Field of Vision, and all parallel Lines which are at right-angles to this Picture Plane will converge to meet at the Vanishing Point.

Two Point Perspective

Two Vanishing Points are established on the Horizon Line in accordance with a 90 degree angle at the base of the assumed position of the artist. This is the Station or Standing Point. The sides of a box, for example, will recede to these points as we perceive the box to be at an angle and showing two of its sides. How much of the top of the box we see will be determined by its height and whether it is above or below the Eye Level (Horizon Line). Every item which is at a different angle will have its own set of Vanishing Points, but they will all share the same Horizon Line.

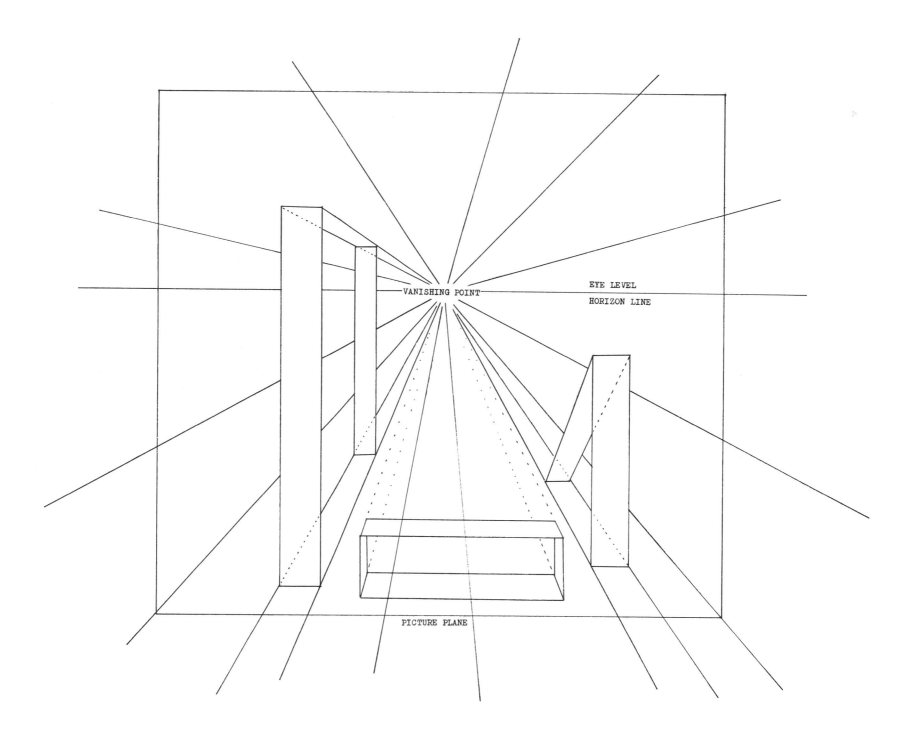

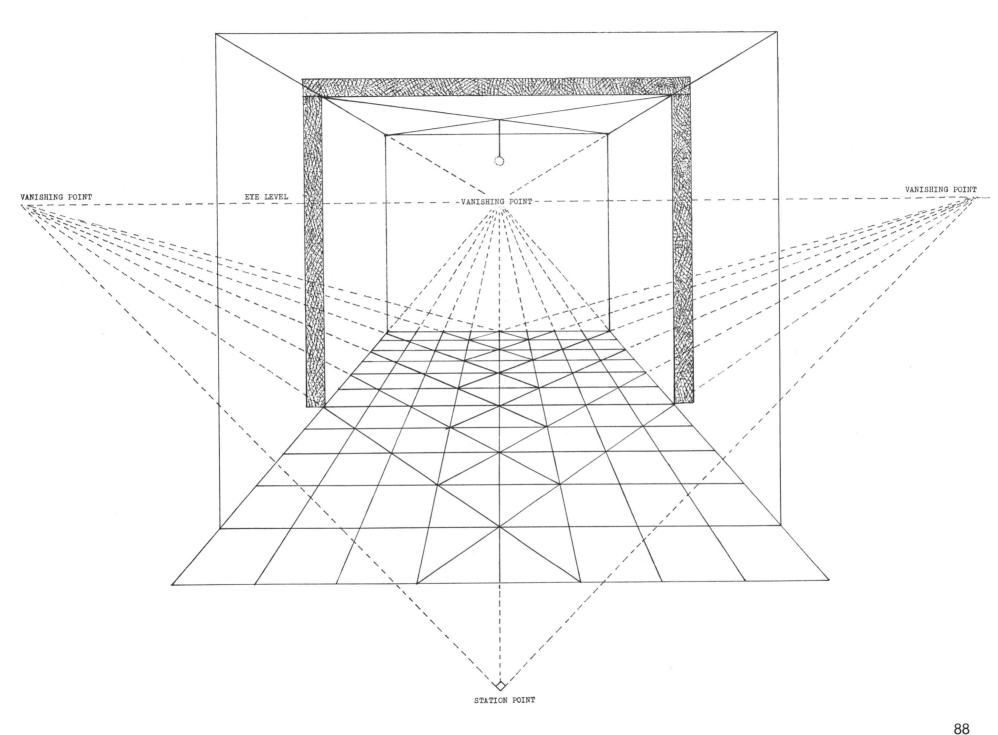

VANISHING POINT

EYE LEVEL

- VANISHING POINT -

VANISHING POINT

STATION POINT

88

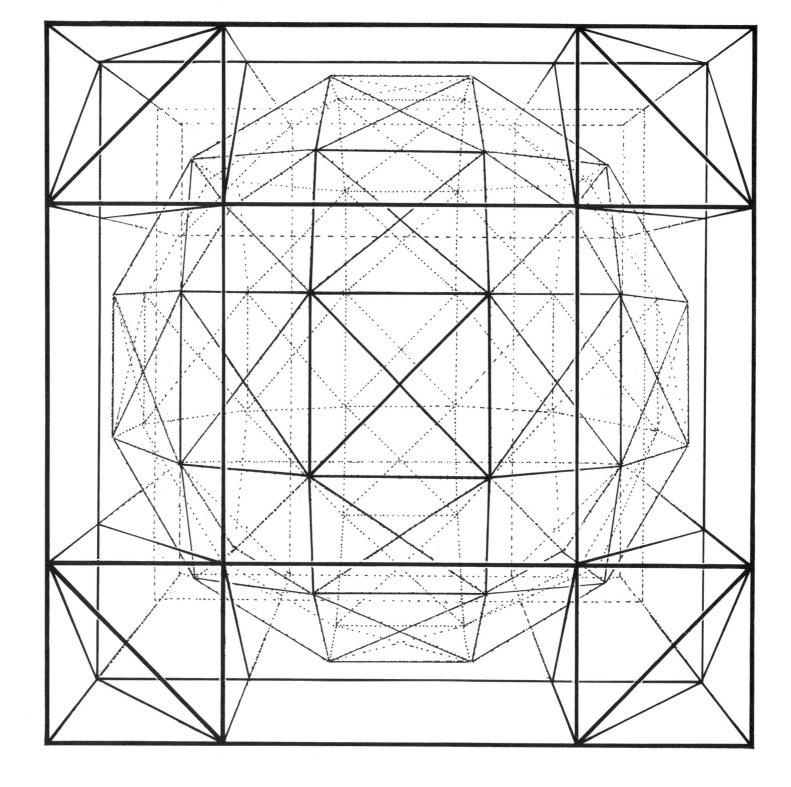

89

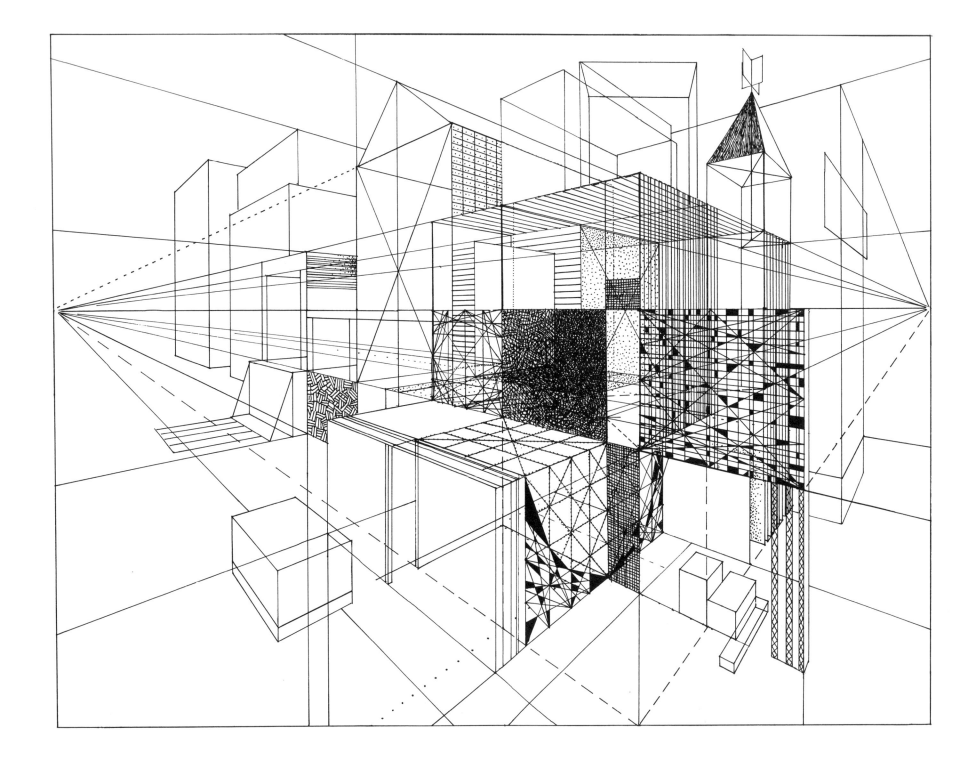

Gary Owen

Three Point Perspective

The vertical Lines of tall buildings often seem to converge in a subtle way to a point somewhere above them, even as their horizontal lines are converging to points on the Horizon Line. Similarly when we look out from a height, vertical lines appear to be converging to a point somewhere below us. The third Vanishing Point is normally determined arbitrarily and adjusted until it 'feels right'. This trial and error method is necessary because the convergence of the lines is so subtle that a great length of paper would be required to actually establish it graphically. This often applies to horizontal Vanishing Points as well. The employment of a third Vanishing Point is most useful when the intention is to emphasize height or depth, and to even dramatize a situation by exaggerating the effects of Perspective.

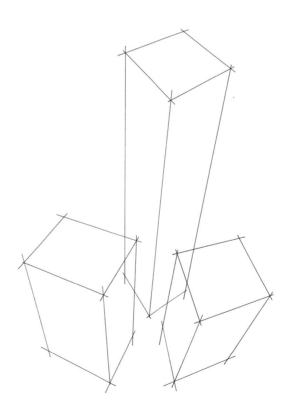

Lise Harvey

93

94

Freehand Perspective

It is possible to measure accurately all the units in a drawing and render a scaled impression of any situation, but the most useful approach to Perspective in drawing is by observation and 'believing our eyes'. If we see some element in Nature as being quite distant and indistinct, we have simply to respond to that and not make it strong and clear in the drawing. Our experience with the relative appearance of things helps to establish them in the drawing and we have simply to be critical of our own work in that regard while the drawing is being developed.

Sensitivity to the qualities of Space and awareness of the 'Natural Laws Concerning Perspective' are really all that one needs to deal successfully with the illusion of depth in a drawing.

Contrasts

Contrasts attract our attention over areas which are more closely related in their tonal values. If black and white are seen together in a particular area, they will appear to be nearer than one which is more middle-tone in quality. A checkered floor pattern is an example. As the black and white squares recede, their relative values weaken, and if taken to an extreme depth, will eventually appear to be the same tone as the lights darken and the darks grow pale. By emphasizing and perhaps exaggerating the speed of this gradation, the sense of Space can be heightened in a drawing of any subject.

Considerable experimenting is necessary to achieve a feeling for Perspective, both through mechanical measurements and freehand methods.

A sense of Space is part of our daily experiences, but when an artist draws our attention to it in a specialized manner, we are reminded that it is an important element in Art as well as in Nature. The suggestion of distant hills behind the Mona Lisa by Da Vinci invites our notice and acknowledgement of them. This makes us even more aware of the figure being close to us and in the foreground. The contrast between the light hills in the distance with the strong figure in the foreground emphasizes the Concept of Space.

In other situations the artist might choose to have the contrasts reversed, with our attention focussed on the light areas as being in the foreground. Rembrandt often employed this approach in his drawings, etchings, and paintings. As suggested earlier, the greater the contrast between the elements, the more noticable and dramatic they will be.

Project Number Thirty-one
Do a drawing in which there is a clear sense of Space behind the subject. To emphasize this feeling, the subject should be drawn fairly large in proportion to its Negative area, and suggestions of Form should be kept to a minimum in order not to attract attention away from the background, which is to be considered the central interest in the drawing through its sense of Space.

Maria Klem

98

Space and Perspective Ideas in a drawing most often seem to concern situations which deal with the feeling of great depth, but actually they concern all aspects of drawing. A head turned slightly away will have one eye nearer to the artist than the other, and one side of the mouth will be nearer than the other. This involves only a small amount of Space, but the appreciation of it will make a great deal of difference in a drawing. These subtleties are every bit as important as those situations of seemingly greater magnitude. A book lying on a table should be drawn with an appreciation of the fact that one end is nearer than the other, and will therefore be slightly clearer and more 'important'. Anything in a drawing which helps to clarify an Idea, in this case 'Space', will share that Idea more directly than if the viewer has to wonder about it.

Perspective is useful when rendering objects in a natural way, but is also a game which can be played with Lines and Shapes in a non-objective manner. If we accept that Space considerations add interest to a drawing then they must also have a use apart from the functional one of depicting things as they might appear in a natural setting. Space suggested through seemingly unnatural elements, such as using only Lines to suggest the Idea of Perspective without actually depicting any particular object, can be fascinating and therefore meaningful.

Decisions about Space must be made by the artist, rather than dictated by the subject which is being drawn. It is common for a drawing to be conceived as flat, with no concern for Ideas of Space. So called 'Primitive Art' seldom deals with Space, but instead all elements are given equal importance and are seen 'up front' in the work. Not only do 'Primitives' tend to keep the surface flat, but many artists consciously strive for that impression. The quality of depth, or the lack of it, in a work must be a conscious decision on the part of the artist.

The intention of the artist regarding Space should be evident in the work, and the viewer should not be in doubt concerning it. As with other Abstract Concepts, the Visual Meaning should communicate clearly regardless of how simple or complex the drawing may be as a whole. When we see the drawing and understand the Visual Idea of it, we will be uplifted in some way.

The work of Magritte, de Chirico, Salvador Dali, Wyeth and Kurelek should be looked at for the use which they have made of Space and Perspective. The control and use of these Concepts will be noticed as very different from that by Matisse, Cezanne, or Odilon Redon.

Susan Kennedy

100

```
         h i
        c a  r
         u
          r
           l
            y                    c
                                  u
                                   r
                                    l
         EYE        e               y
        s                          h
       o                        a
      n               a        i
                       r          r
         mout h

          c
         h i n
              e
              c
              k
```

curly hair

curly hair

EYE

ear

nose

mouth

chin

neck

Chapter Six

INFORMATION

as an Abstract Concept

Anything which a drawing displays or emphasizes is 'telling' something about the subject as well as about the interests of the artist. Beyond initially identifying the subject, the drawing may show a great deal of Information, or very little, much like the strip-tease dancer. When some things are held back and not shown our imagination is encouraged to play an active role, whereas when we are shown everything there is nothing left for the imagination, and we become less interested.

Information in a drawing is an 'active' element, while those areas which are contributing very little to the drawing Idea are considered 'passive'. These two elements play a role similar to Positive and Negative aspects, and are as important. A passive area allows the eye to rest and also gives the imagination opportunity to become involved. The active area involves the eye directly by giving it the Information as provided by the artist. The artist must be in control of both aspects.

The subject matter which an artist may be using in a drawing presents itself as having more to it than cold facts about proportions or other apparent features. The light quality, effects of the environment, mood, and meaningfulness are all equally important considerations from a Visual point of view. The artist should always be aware of the many possibilities available in perhaps even a simple setting, and be able to select particular aspects of it.

An old chair may have an interesting Shape, and we may be inspired to draw it because of our attraction to that aspect of it. All that seems necessary for the drawing to be satisfying, apart from the enjoyment of actually doing it, is to capture the Idea of its Shape. If the drawing is not completely accurate in every detail, have we failed and wasted our time? Not at all, because the original Idea was not to render it photographically, and the drawing reflects the interest in the Shape of the chair as an emotional involvement. The Information provided includes the Idea of the chair, and also the feeling put into the drawing of it.

The amount, quality, and selection of the Information content bears directly on the nature of the intended Expression. If a drawing is meant to depict a swan, but in fact leaves the viewer in doubt as to what kind of bird it is, due to inaccuracies in the Shape, the Idea is not successfully communicated. If a figure is intended to represent a dance movement, but appears to be simply walking, then again there is a failure to communicate the intended Idea due to incorrect Information.

A Shape alone may identify the subject and what it is doing simply by displaying a basic amount of Information. Loose configurations can suggest for us a bird, figure, or a non-objective Idea, and our response will relate to the particular suggestion. Even a casual reference to distant hills in a drawing may be very satisfying and encourage our imagination to become involved. The task of the artist is to ensure that the Information which the drawing does contain is communicating in the intended manner to the viewer.

Project Number Thirty-two
Do a drawing in which various elements of Information are emphasized. Do several drawings of the same subject, each time focussing on a different aspect of it.

Suzanne Clark-Thompson

An artist may be inclined to draw in a very realistic manner, and therefore be concerned with every possible aspect of Information about the subject. In this case the actual choice of subject matter may not be a crucial factor because the illusion of reality can be invoked with any setting. The involvement is with 'illusion', rather than concern for a particular subject. The intention would not be to make something look beautiful or otherwise interesting, but rather to make it look as real as possible within the limitations of the drawing materials which are used.

To draw with the prime interest being the achievement of a realistic impression of a subject and its environment, and to successfully convey a true sense of reality on the two-dimensional drawing surface, would inspire a sense of magic and wonderment. The challenge to the artist is to instill an energy and tension into the drawing so that it becomes a clear Expression itself, and not simply a duplication or copy of the subject. As with other approaches, the drawing must be the interesting thing in the end, quite apart from whether or not the subject itself is accurately rendered.

A photograph of a beautiful model is no guarantee that it will turn out to be a good picture. The photographer must be in control of the lighting, atmosphere, general mood, and the composition. A photograph which is aesthetically pleasing is as much a tribute to the photographer as it is to the subject. The camera records the Information which the photographer wishes it to record, and in what degree, according to the importance of it in relation to the Idea for the picture. On the other hand, a passport photo is simply intended to be cold Information, and as a result is seldom aesthetically pleasing to anyone.

'Aesthetically pleasing', 'interesting', 'disturbing', or 'intriguing' can each refer to many things about a work of Art. Reference may be to the atmosphere or general mood of the piece, its Composition, style, or subject matter. The Information provided in the work will control its overall impression, and for this reason plays a very important role.

Project Number Thirty-three
Do a drawing in which every aspect of the subject is depicted as accurately as possible. Consider every detail which concerns the subject, such as the quality of light, surface Textures etc. Try to instill a real sense of life into the drawing and not be satisfied with a cold factual rendering for its own sake.

Doug Dunford

107

Showing the effects of strong sunlight on people and buildings, and the mood of tranquility it can convey, was a major element in the work of Edward Hopper. William Turner, in another part of the world at a different time was also deeply impressed by the effects of the sun, but he took from it the sense of drama which had been imprinted on his imagination. How things such as the sun, trees, or infinite Space affect us is bound to influence our outlook and our work. Since communication of feelings is as important to the artist as to the poet, this becomes an element of vital Information in the work itself.

Putting Information about feelings down on paper as a Visual image requires initially the intention of the artist to give that aspect a dominant role in the work. The artist must create the means of communicating the Idea and Information about the feelings, as there is no definitive way to show them in Visual terms. A model may be soft spoken and have delicate features, but if the artist felt her to be a 'hard' person, a drawing using crisp, strong Lines may convey the feelings of the artist more accurately than drawing the purely Visual aspects of the model. Putting 'feeling' into a drawing as part of the Information content is often difficult because of its spontaneous and fleeting nature, but the artist must try to take hold of it and make it a part of a general vocabulary of drawing possibilities.

Project Number Thirty-four
Do several drawings which convey Information about particular feelings or impressions.

When the artist puts special qualities into a drawing, whether they be exaggerations for dramatic effects, or other Ideas intended to evoke emotional responses, they automatically become part of the Information content of the work because we are being made aware of them. Like anything else, Information must be selected and given emphasis if it is to be communicated to others as well as have real meaning for the artist. These elements must be organized and given importance in relation to the interest the artist wishes them to have.

Doug Dunford

108

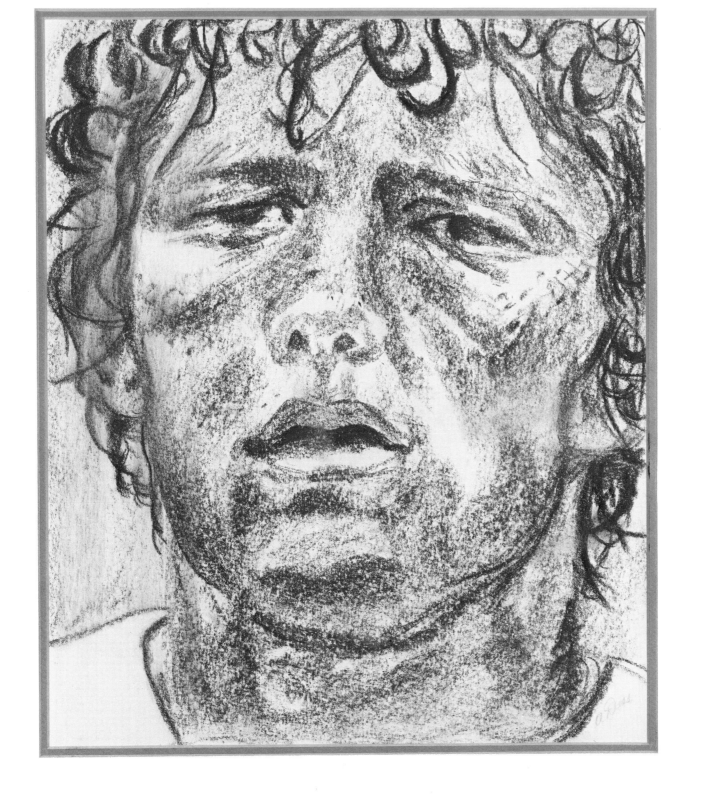

Anita Dees

110

Sometimes the subject itself has connotations which are familiar to a great many people and in this case the Information is centred on the Literal Meaning in the work. Drawings of immediately recognizable faces such as that of Terry Fox or Marilyn Monroe have an impact and evoke feelings of sadness or nostalgia. Goya's 'Horrors of War' show what their title suggests and they display a lot of cruel Information. Greg Curnoe's 'C N Tower' evokes a thought about contemporary values. The 'shock of recognition' is an emotion in itself and is further exemplified in Oldenburg's 'Clothes-Pin' which he constructed as a piece of sculpture several feet high. His large drawings of cigarette butts are also familiar items not previously considered worthy of being a subject for a work of Art.

There is room in Art for nostalgia, and even a touch of humour which occurs when we see ordinary things 'glorified'.

Project Number Thirty-five

Do several drawings larger than life of familiar objects. They should be clearly drawn for instant recognition by any viewer. Try to 'glorify' these drawings of things which you might not have considered before as subjects to draw.

Drawing has long played the role of being the Information Gatherer for artists, much as note-taking is for the newspaper reporter. An artist may want to jot down Ideas for use as reference material for future works. The act of making these drawings also strengthens the impression the subject may have had on the artist. The act of drawing must always be an enjoyable involvement if one is to continue with it, and although Information may be collected along the way, the activity of drawing is often the central motivating force or emotional release for the artist. To draw solely for the purpose of gathering Information is only an exercise in observation which will be frustrating and fruitless if it isn't enjoyable. Information for its own sake can be cold and empty.

Information must be selected for its sympathy towards the subject, and this becomes an element of input from the artist. He or she may choose to overlook certain aspects in favour of others found to be more interesting. However, Visual characteristics are important in determining the role of Information in a drawing and therefore the artist must establish priorities at the outset. For example, a model's eyes might be more attracting to the artist than the clothes she is wearing, and will therefore receive a greater amount of attention in the drawing. The situation may also be the other way around where the clothes become the dominant factor with the features of lesser importance. Also a subject may be highly patterned, but if the Information passed on through the drawing is that of purely its Shape, the drawing will in fact be missing the more pertinent aspects of the subject. However, it is the artist's choice which aspects to use, and which to disregard.

A non-objective drawing containing Shapes and Lines is conveying the Information about those elements and the amount supplied through the artist's imagination or creativity is determined by that artist. Information has to do with what the drawing is about. If it is about Shapes, or about Lines, or about quick brush strokes, it is all pertinent to the understanding of it. These elements can be 'subject matter' in that they constitute what the drawing is concerned with.

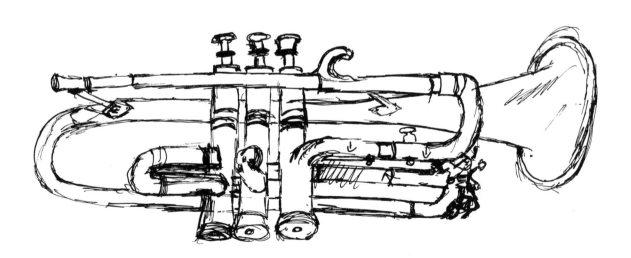

Paddy Ormiston

112

Gwen Kirk

113

A written letter contains Information in the words but it is the Visual quality of the writing which provides the aesthetic pleasure of the letter. Information without the accompaniment of aesthetic considerations cannot make an interesting drawing. The selection and use of the Information aspect of a drawing or other work of Art is always important however, for it sets the tone of the work as a whole. Generally speaking, it presents what the drawing is about and therefore is a factor which can never be overlooked.

Artists owe it to themselves to be aware of all Visual possibilities and not be confined to a narrow few. Information about light quality, Form, Shape, feeling etc., are all equally important but the artist must control their effects in the drawing. It is how the Information communicates through the drawing in accordance with the intended Expression which matters most in the end.

Barry Shelton

115

Veronica Taylor

Chapter Seven

COMPOSITION
as an Abstract Concept

A Composition is a creation which exists within a defined area. It is a complete unit and is what the creative endeavour is focussed on. Music and Poetry have a beginning and an end, while Art has borders within which to express an Idea, and to which it must relate.

As with Music and Poetry, there are many ways to approach the issue of Composition, and there are many reliable structures as well as freedoms available to the artist.

By definition, a Composition refers to the sum total of its parts and it is how these parts come together or are organized that dictates the strength or weakness of a drawing. The given structures are those settings which have been proven over many generations to be effective and which make the best use of the limitations imposed by a defined area.

Sometimes when a drawing seems comfortable on a page we may not be conscious of a Composition plan at all. This is a desired effect for it means that the drawing is harmoniously organized and is meaningful as a result. The Composition Idea or 'plan' is an integral part of the overall drawing Idea for it concerns the entire area and represents a non-objective, organizational aspect of a work of Art. This is as vital to Andrew Wyeth as to **Vasarely**.

Zoltan Markan

There are conditions under which a poem or a tune are best appreciated, and the same applies for a drawing. A matte placed around it will clarify the drawing as being a complete entity with a clearly defined area. To carry this idea further, when it is placed in a frame and positioned on a wall in a home, the drawing may then be viewed and appreciated to advantage.

No formula exists which can replace personal feelings and intuition regarding a particular Idea, and therefore an experimental attitude and a trial and error approach are often prime assets for an artist to have and to develop. The various approaches discussed on the following pages are intended to encourage the conscious consideration of the whole drawing area through a suggested structure in each case, but special interests which the artist may want to explore are also encouraged.

Drawing in general does not have the same demands put upon it regarding Composition as does painting, but an awareness of the potentials of Composition is essential. Theories regarding it will naturally relate to painting and design as well. Composition is what gives structure to a work, without which a drawing will invariably appear to be weak and unresolved.

An important first step is to establish the perimeters at the outset by defining them in a firm manner with the same material which is being used for the drawing. This provides an original border rather than the one dictated by the size and Shape of the paper. Whether or not a drawn border is employed in every instance, the central issue is that the entire area be considered.

Jane Everard

Composition Number One

Positive and Negative

When the drawing is composed of two sections which can be horizontal, vertical, irregular etc., one should 'read' as Positive, the other as Negative. The proportions involved are important and play a major role in determining the Visual interest which results. The two sections should complement each other rather than 'fight', and this is best achieved when one is dominant and the other of a more quiet nature.

The smaller of the two sections need not necessarily be the Negative, or passive area. If it is treated in an active manner, making it meaningful and more visually attracting than the larger area, it will be read as the Positive part of the drawing. For example, if horizontal sections were considered to represent a landscape, the amount of area for the sky as opposed to that of the land will naturally influence the mood of the work. The sky may be active with Textures, clouds etc., or quiet and subtle. The land may also be either very active with details, Textures, etc., or very uniform and quiet, allowing the upper section, sky, to be the dominant interest.

It should be observed that the Mona Lisa by Da Vinci is basically a Composition containing two distinct sections. The figure in the foreground is clearly the Positive attraction with the background allowed to fade into the distance. The Shape of the foreground is very agreeable in proportion to the Shape of the Negative section, and although our attention is held with the figure, there are subtle elements of interest in the background if we choose to look for them. There is no distinct division between the hills and sky, for if there were, the Idea of the background being a unified Shape would be weakened.

Being aware of the possibilities and value of various approaches to Composition is the important first step.

Monica Shelton

Composition Number Two

Multiple Divisions

When a drawing contains both vertical and horizontal divisions the Composition becomes more complex. The artist must work out the relationships both of Shape and proportions as well as Positive and Negative attractions. When the Lines and Shapes reach to the borders as they do when the Composition is 'divided', the eye is also led to the edges and may in imagination go out and beyond those borders.

When interest is carried to the edge of the drawing, a certain tension is created at that point. This situation is frustrated when the Line or Shape stops just short of the edge, or seems to touch it rather than meeting the border in a firm manner. If the Composition Idea is purely Positive and Negative in nature, and only of two sections, the tension at the border is balanced on either side in a comfortable way. However when the Composition is more complex, the artist must be aware of the attracting nature of tensions at the edges and counter them in some way in order not to upset the general balance of the drawing.

'Whistler's Mother' is a familiar painting which demonstrates this approach to Composition, but there are also many similar examples in the works of Vermeer, Seurat, Mondrian, Motherwell, and Andrew Wyeth. Cezanne developed many works in this manner as well and is known as a 'great Composer'. His approach to Art was to paint paintings, not 'things'. The objects which he used were simply devices chosen for their usefulness in his experiments with constructing a work of Art in a rational way. It is often a difficult thing to accept that the objects themselves are not the most important part of a work.

Composition Number Three

Self-Contained

Creating a Composition which does NOT lead the eye to the perimeter of the drawing is perhaps the most common approach. Instead the attention is held within the drawing area in a forthright manner. The most basic method to accomplish this is to draw with a contrasting material, and the attention automatically goes to where the drawing is. Decisions by the artist as to where the eye is to be directed remain important, for the eye must be led to some part of the drawing if there is to be any sense of structure.

Composition involves structure, and this involves a control over those areas which attract attention and appreciating the value of Negative areas. If there seems to be no sense of order, an unsettling situation will exist as it does when in Music there seems to be no sense of relationship between the notes which are played. The areas of attraction must appear to have a purpose in relation to the whole.

A conscious control over areas designated as 'interests' is important, for if everything in the drawing were to demand equal attention a sense of chaos could exist. Similarly if nothing seems to be of particular interest, no interest in the drawing by the viewer will likely be the result.

To achieve a Self-Contained Composition, manipulation of the elements in the drawing is often necessary. Lines must not be allowed to carry undue attention to the border areas, and so movements relating to the edges is more the requirement in this case. A simple analogy is a circle within a square, where the Lines of the circle flow in a direction which relate to those of the square. The attention would be even more focussed on the circle if the area between it and the square were darkened.

Attention can be held in the drawing by the use of tone as in the above example, or by the use of a linear quality which flows in relation to the borders. As with other approaches to Composition, a resolve on the part of the artist is the prime ingredient, and is apparent in the finished work. In Constable's painting entitled 'Salisbury Cathedral' he manipulated the lines of the trees and other Shapes in the foreground in order that our attention could not help but go to the cathedral in the centre. This manipulation is also seen in the work of Rembrandt, and the self-contained Composition is virtually his trade-mark. For this reason a study of his methods is essential.

A drawing can also create its own Shape and feel to be a complete unit or Composition. It must be assumed that a drawing does not necessarily have to be rectangular, but can take a less geometric Shape when this relates better to the Idea of the artist. However, even in this case the attention must be held In the drawing, and therefore the Shape of it must not be so interesting as to take interest away from the central area.

Whenever the interest is clearly held within the Composition, regardless of how simple or complex the actual work is, it will be understood to be the intention of the artist. Picasso's 'Guernica', and Rothko's series of Colour impressions are examples of contrasting Visual Ideas which share a common Composition Idea, although it may not be immediately apparent.

Composition Number Four

Repetition

When there is more than one 'centre of interest' which relate to each other in some way, the attention of the viewer is allowed to drift from one to the other and can appreciate the repeated effect. Seeing things in groups of two or more is common in our daily experiences, as we think of two eyes, two arms, three kittens, seven people in a restaurant, etc. so it seems natural to have similar situations appear as the Idea in a work of Art.

Several objects may in fact appear as one Shape if they are in a tight grouping, or they may be spaced in a variety of ways. Attention to the Negative space between the objects is important for it directly affects the mood of the work.

When the spaces are organized as the windows of a building, or buttons on a blouse the predictability becomes part of the structure. The items in this case are similar, and the spaces between them are also a repeated element. These predictable situations, or patterns, are familiar to us, and they have their individual functions both in Art and in real life for they provide a sense of stability and organization, both practically and visually.

On the other hand, if we were to see flowers in a vase neatly arranged so that they have equal spaces, and if the flowers themselves were identical to each other, we would feel uncomfortable with this obviously calculated setting. Although we are accustomed to seeing groups of flowers, we know that they are individual items and are meant to be appreciated as such. Nor would they be evenly spaced. Similarly we would not expect to see people on a beach equally spaced and looking all the same.

When there is more than one, the items reinforce the individual nature of the other, as with a male and female. The differences can be readily appreciated, but the similarities create an obvious relationship. There would be an interest not evident if there was only one figure in the drawing.

The nature of the repeated element varies from one drawing to another. In some cases it may be the general area of the Shapes, or the Negative spaces. In another it may be the repeated nature of the technique employed for the drawing such as consistent vertical Lines. The important factor remains the appreciation of the value of repeated elements for their ability to create a special interest which results when there is 'more than one'.

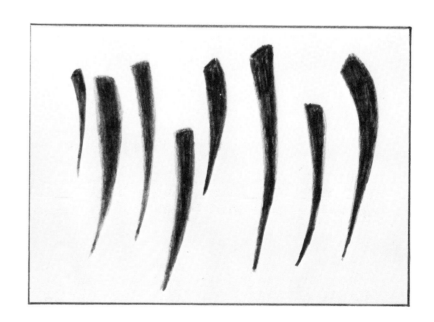

SKY RHYTHMS

Conyers Barker

130

Composition Number Five

Rhythm

Unbroken Lines which flow and undulate across the page set up an unmistakeable sense of rhythm which can be related to rolling hills, drifting clouds, or a reclining figure. The impression created is one of peacefulness and movement. Flowing Lines would not be used by someone wishing to evoke a sense of rigidity or discord.

Emphasis on the flowing nature of Shapes and Lines involves manipulating and elongating elements until a desired effect is achieved. If Van Gogh drew the cypress trees as he saw them, rather than how he felt them and their relationship with the hills and sky, we would not have his 'Starry Night'. The flowing movement throughout the work combines the elements into a rhythmic whole.

A sense of movement encourages the viewer to become involved with the work rather than remain a passive observer. Sensitivity on the part of the artist towards the inter-relationship of the parts of a Composition is important, in order to take advantage of them and set up a flowing movement. Modigliani achieved his Visual rhythm by being aware of the possibility of it, and then adopting it as part of his central Idea.

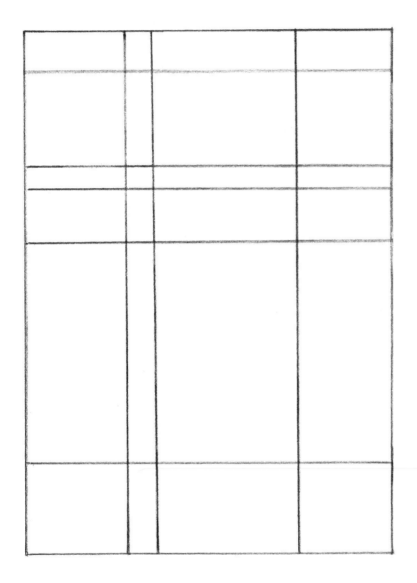

Composition Number Six

Harmony

Harmony occurs in a work where there are common elements which inter-relate. This can involve Textures, Shapes, Forms, or Lines which are used in the drawing. Sharing a common technical approach, such as short pen strokes, will also create a harmonious impression.

In the cause of harmony, objects or Shapes must often be simplified and given common components which may at times seem contrary to their essential nature. A still-life, figure, or non-objective Shapes can be rendered, for example, entirely with straight Lines and since the sides of the drawing are also straight, no conflict can exist.

One must look for common elements for, like rhythm, they do exist in Nature, and are but to be appreciated and employed in Art. Sharing a light source, common ground, etc., and people who share a common philosophy form natural groupings. One must simply be aware of what harmony can do for a drawing.

Harmony in a drawing is agreeable to the eyes of the viewer. When there is nothing to upset or counteract the impression of natural inter-relationships between all segments of a drawing, regardless of the subject matter, it will be comfortable to look at.

The message in Goya's 'Horrors of War' series is one of violence but the Visual harmony and attention to artistic concerns is what causes them to be appreciated as works of Art. Perhaps it is because of their harmony in Visual terms which accounts for the strength of their Literal Message, due to the seeming contradictions which are presented.

Composition Number Seven

Tension

Tension occurs when something seems to be unrelated to an existing situation, or when some aspects of Information are withheld. Where harmony presents a certain comfortable setting, tension causes the viewer to be momentarily startled or arrested, much like a horizontal Line is arrested when it meets with a vertical Line. Harmony allows one to relax and take things for granted, while tension in a drawing keeps one alert because there are fewer predictable features.

A circle within a circle presents a related and comfortable setting, while a circle within a square presents an uneasy calm with its contrasting elements which oblige the viewer to consider it in a different way. This tension must be understood to be a healthy and desireable element when employed to create interest, keeping things from becoming dull.

Unusual or otherwise unexpected situations such as a drawing depicting a head with an unusually long nose, or a figure seeming to float in space, cause tension and create interest. Anything which is different from what might be consciously or sub-consciously expected obliges the viewer to become involved in the contemplation of it.

When the artist wants the viewer to become actively involved and to evoke some form of response, tension is employed. Intrique is a subtle form of tension which occurs when the viewer is left in doubt about something which is merely hinted at, such as only part of a Shape drawn in or other situations which are deliberately created by the artist to cause puzzlement.

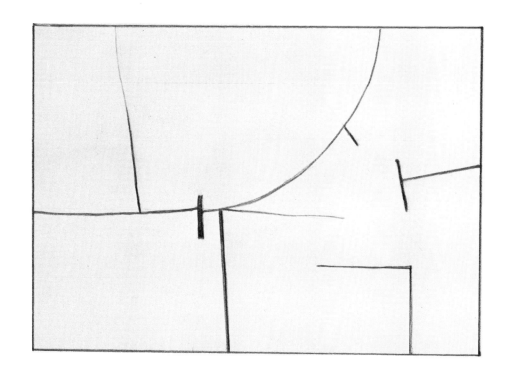

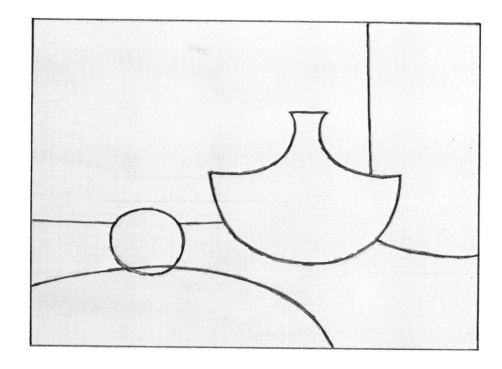

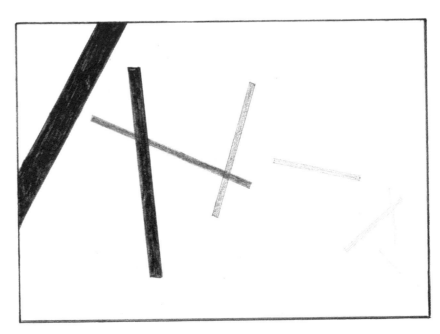

Composition Number Eight

Space

Awareness of Space is part of our everyday experience and looking into the distance is related to absorbing some of Nature's grandeur where one is inspired to contemplate the meaning of things or find a feeling of peacefulness. It follows that Space as an Idea for a Composition will be a natural element in Art. The means to create a sense of Space are available to the artist and the simple requirement is to regard the drawing surface as if it were Space. This frees the artist from the assumed restrictions normally imposed by a 'flat surface'.

The Visual effects of Space and Form as viewed in our normal surroundings are usually very subtle, especially when only a short distance is involved. The artist must exaggerate these effects in order to clarify the Idea in the work. There is no misunderstanding regarding Space in the Art of Breughel, Rosa **Bonheur**, Magritte, Dali, or Wyeth, but it must also be appreciated that these artists used its effects to their own ends. A different use of Space is evident in the works of Klee or Gottleib where they are seldom felt to be 'flat', but instead seem alive with a Space of their own.

Considerations regarding Space are equally important when the Idea is to keep the drawing 'flat'. This may appear simple because the surface is flat to begin with, but a feeling of Space develops whenever there are contrasts and one section feels to be closer than another. The relative positions must be kept under control by the artist whether the Idea is to suggest Space or to keep the Idea flat.

The use of Space is often related to the argument that Art should not deal with illusions, but be a statement in itself, without reference to natural phenomena. The truth is that Space impressions are always occuring in a work of Art, as some things will feel to be close and other things seem to be farther away, regardless of the subject or non-objective Idea. It is the artist's task to remain in control of it.

Composition Number Nine

Leading The Eye

Attracting the attention of the viewer to one area, and then leading it gently to another, provides movement and involvement in a playful sense. Flowing Lines which may suggest winding rivers, or an arrow Shape pointing in some direction will encourage the eye to follow the intended Idea. A pointing finger, or glancing eyes can also direct attention from one area to another, and if there is something for the eye to pick up on once it has followed the intended lead, it will feel rewarded.

A Composition should not be conceived as a static thing, but one which is alive, and encourages the viewer to participate. Areas of tension and contrast will attract the eye initially, but secondary interests must be provided in order to give the eye somewhere to go following the first seed of interest in the drawing. A headline in a newspaper will catch our interest, but the succeeding article must be there to satisfy our need for more Information as our eyes seek out and follow along with the story. A static headline is not enough to satisfy this need on its own.

If we see a drawing of a figure in which there is no clear attracting area, we will be left with the difficult task of appreciating the whole drawing at once. This could be effective if the Shape of the entire figure is striking in some way, but if it also displays no special features, the drawing will be unsatisfying.

On the other hand, when an area such as an eye, or a hand, or a shoulder, attracts the initial attention, and we are led on to other areas in a clear manner we feel encouraged to follow the lead and derive more satisfaction from the drawing.

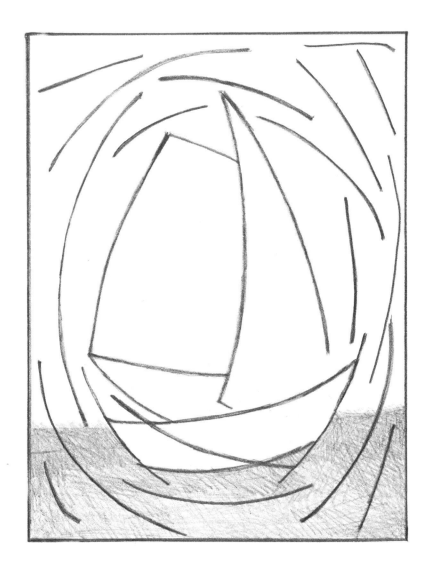

140

Composition Number Ten

Combinations

Each Composition Idea has unique qualities, and can enrichen the effects of others when combined in a sensitive manner in a drawing or other work of Art. However the artist must be wary of the dangers of possibly producing a negative effect by combining two or more Ideas which are very different from each other. To combine a 'divided' Idea with a 'self-contained' Composition would present an immediate conflict because of their obvious differences. One or the other should be dominant, with a slight amount of 'conflict' adding tension and interest to the work.

The value of Composition Ideas is to provide 'order' in place of 'chaos', and to encourage the viewer into contemplation of the work by presenting the invitation through being visually enticing. An examination of the Art of Breughel, Cezanne, Bonnard, Wyeth, Warhol, Colville, Jock MacDonald, and others who present strong works is a necessary learning experience into Composition Ideas.

As mentioned earlier, nothing can replace personal motivation and intuitive Ideas, but these must also be tempered with a consideration of the whole surface. Rational thinking about balance and impact of the Idea is also a necessary activity. Awareness of the existence of various approaches to a 'problem' help one to find their own most comfortable means of Expression through Composition. **Mondrian found his, and so did Dali.**

A Composition Idea is as important as the Visual Idea of a drawing because it is what we see as a first impression. It involves the whole drawing, and is expected to be interesting in some way. There are many approaches and variations which are possible, and the artist has but to explore them and to exploit them. It is not enough to duplicate the Composition Ideas of others, for one must be creative and provide his or her own kind of structure and meaning to the make-up of a work of Art.

Janis Gadowski

142

Pierrette Scanlan

Chapter Eight

EXPRESSION
as an Abstract Concept

A musician expresses himself through sound, a dancer through body movements, and an artist through images. This Expression is a manifestation in concrete terms of a personal Idea or feeling.

Artists in the past have fought for this freedom of Expression, and we are the beneficiaries. Today personal Expression in Art is encouraged at every level as it is acknowledged that Art is more than decorative items to hang on a wall, illustrate a story, or perpetuate a tradition. Drawing can involve our sense of sight in an emotional way and convey a feeling of purpose in its own right.

Visual Expression directly affects the use made of all other Abstract Concepts because it embodies the central Idea of the artist. It may be obvious or subtle, but for a drawing to be alive with its own energy, this conscious input from the artist is essential. A drawing may be accurate but lifeless if it only has the functional use of depicting some object.

A coffee cup is fundamentally required to be useful, but we are also affected by its Shape as well as its other Visual aspects. In drawing, a Line may serve a functional purpose when used to define a Shape, but it can also have a life of its own if it possesses interesting expressive qualities. A drawing of a head may also be considered basically functional, but if it has unique aspects such as apparent distortion of the features it will have more Visual Meaning than a coldly accurate rendering of the subject. The creative input from an artist becomes the essence of a work in aesthetic terms.

The role of Art is not to duplicate Nature but to create new works which are visually meaningful. To try to mirror the soft qualities of a model by 'copying' them with pen and ink would be futile. The drawing must be meaningful in its own way. The crisp clean Lines of the pen have their own virtues which may at some point combine with those of the model, but are in essence quite separate. A drawing may reflect Ideas about Nature, as will a photograph, but their success will depend on how they interest us visually through their special qualities.

The desire to draw meaningfully is a natural thing for anyone interested in drawing, and one does not have to 'learn to draw' first. Developing an appreciation of Visual Ideas is essential to learning what drawing is all about, and this can come only through their use from the beginning.

Everyone has Ideas, but not everyone does something about them. In Art, an Idea which is not realized visually is no Idea at all because there is nothing to look at. Thoughts develop from Ideas and drawings which have preceded them, and then go on to affect other drawings. It is hard to imagine what we would have if Rembrandt or Picasso had done only a few sketches, or if Paul Klee had tried out only one or two Ideas.

Visual Expression relates to a person's general preferences in Art as well as to spontaneous feelings, but no Idea is necessarily more valid than another. The artist must put them down on paper in a resolute way to his or her own satisfaction, keeping in mind the creating of something which did not exist before.

The physical involvement of the artist ceases to be a part of the drawing as soon as it is completed, for then it must have its own life and be judged accordingly. The frame of mind the artist may have been in, or the nature of the environment at the time, will not affect our appreciation of the work itself. The expressive drawings and paintings of Van Gogh stand on their own energy, and it is difficult to relate them to the personal troubles which he had. He shared his vibrant thoughts with us, but not his problems.

Derek Martin

An artist may want to share his feelings about something which interests and excites him, or simply want to experiment with Visual effects to make them meaningful. Attempting to make a work have its own energy by employing some form of Abstract Concept is where the real enjoyment of drawing lies. It also takes on a greater personal meaning when there is some feeling and thought put into the drawing.

How a drawing is done directly affects our response to it, and for that reason we can get several different impressions from drawings of the same subject by the same artist if each conveys a different Visual Idea. Each approach has a personality of its own, whether that be a strong sense of Form, the use of expressive Lines, or even a drawing in a highly realistic manner. The artist has successfully expressed Ideas when we are able to understand and relate to them without written Information or titles. That is all the viewer asks of the artist.

June Chambers

Sharon Webster

Patty Hill

To depict emotions such as anger, happiness, or melancholy is more difficult than drawing objects. However, the jagged Shapes and sombre tones in Picasso's 'Guernica' leave one in no doubt as to the intended Expression of the work. The tortured features and distortions become unsettling and moving at the same time. The consistency of the 'angry' Shapes and the tonal structure, present a strong statement in Visual terms about the agony of repression. Edvard Munch's 'The Scream', and the moving drawings of Kathe Kollwitz are also excellent examples of that kind of Expression in Art. The clear use of Form and the solid Shapes of the figures combine with the suggested activity of the figures to present an impression of pathos and desperation which make it impossible to be mistaken for 'pleasant sketches'. The need to express honest earthly emotions is a natural thing, but to discover how best to do it in a Visual manner must be for the individual artist to resolve.

Artistic Expression is not always as personal as we might like to think. Our environment affects us a great deal, and so does what we have been taught to believe about Art. How we think of things is often a reflection of how others have thought, and as a result we may not actually know what we think ourselves. There have always been philosophies and Schools of Art which tend to form public opinion, and conforming to these is sometimes felt to be necessary to gain acceptance and general appreciation. A frame-work within which to work is often helpful, but can have a negative effect if artists do not take up the challenge to engage in their own Ideas and have honest feelings about what they do.

How one feels about things and personal interests should directly influence one's work. We know what interested Emily Carr, Edward Hopper, Marc Rothko, Paul Klee, and William Kurelek. No one has to apologize for preferences in Art, but instead should feel encouraged to pursue them and explore one's own true interests with a passion. Only then will the work possess the strong, central Ideas so necessary to meaningful drawing. Personal Expression takes drawing beyond the confines of predictability, and sometimes respectability.

Chapter Nine

Idioms and Ideas

The refinement which occurs after many generations of working within a traditional framework is evident in the Art of Ancient Egypt, Greece, Africa, etc. Cultural groups seem to develop a natural, collective mode of Expression and although individual artists may be identified because of special skills, their work continues to reflect the style of the culture. There are well known Inuit, Japanese, Mexican, and American artists who have recognizable styles, but whose work nevertheless bears the general trademark of their culture.

The influence of one's heritage is strong, and artists have often tried to break from it by escaping to other countries or by rejecting it in other ways. Most have come back to the realization that their heritage is part of themselves, and that being true to one is being true to the other. Personal styles can develop within the broader scope of a cultural mode of Expression and contribute to it in a meaningful way.

However, in the contemporary world where mass communication and world-wide travel possibilities create a sense of international consciousness regarding artistic philosophies, international cultural groups which recognize no geographic barriers tend to form. The influence of the group philosophy is evident in the work of the individual members who have joined together in a common bond of a shared philosophical approach. Working within such an adopted framework provides moral support for the members of this 'new culture'. There were no national boundaries to Impressionism, Abstract Expressionism, or Surrealism, nor are there boundaries to Conceptual Art. At present in the world there are many internationally recognized Idioms, or modes of Expression, whose adherents are found in almost every country.

There have always been (and probably always will be) collective or cultural styles of either national or international flavour. Equally there have always been individuals whose work stands out as being unique and unaligned to any group philosophy. Sometimes this occurs within a cultural setting, as with Michelangelo during the Renaissance movement in Italy, or Andrew Wyeth in the school of Realism. Nonetheless they are thought of as individuals along with Rembrandt, Vermeer, Breughel, Da Vinci, Turner, Van Gogh, Klee, Miro, Picasso, etc., and their work seems to have universal appeal and a timelessness which matches that of cultural forces.

The structure and feelings of confidence and inspiration displayed by individual works, whether or not they are part of a larger cultural Idiom, serve as a measuring stick for what Art is capable of achieving, along with being a moving experience. They should also remind us of our own freedoms and individuality.

When we see tin cans turned into meaningful sculptures by Viktor Tinkl, or dancing girls in their high-heeled shoes expressively drawn by Robert Markle, or High Realism by Ken Danby, we should not try to emulate them. Instead we should be inspired to explore our own potential as creative individuals.

A characteristic means of Expression seems to develop naturally when an artist comes to terms with his or her own interests and preferences. It becomes refined into a meaningful style only after much exploration and repetition through a large number of works. The personality in the work begins to surface and communication becomes effective when reinforced through a body of work and over a period of time.

Personal approaches must be nurtured and encouraged for the uniqueness which they possess, rather than put down as undesirable or unimportant. Pressures to conform to accepted Idioms are either imaginary or real, but most often negative in effect. One must be aware of his or her own individuality and make choices based on personal introspection while allowing others their individuality as well.

The need to communicate through Visual means is closely linked to the enjoyment and personal satisfactions derived through the activity itself. Working out an Idea on paper and developing it into a meaningful entity is possibly the most exciting part. Contemplation of the finished work by the artist is often anti-climactic, and for continued fulfillment one must go on to produce other works. The artist will be encouraged if the work elicits positive reactions from others, but must be strong enough to believe in his or her own Ideas even if others do not. This may be considered self-indulgent, but is in fact the honest approach. To desire and need some form of understanding and appreciation from others is natural, but the perseverance and integrity demanded of the artist is also an important issue.

Decisions regarding the kind of reaction desired by the artist are an important part of the motivation and will naturally influence the approach to the work. An artist may want to startle the viewer either through a choice of a controversial subject matter or by means of an obviously novel way of drawing a subject which may in itself be quite commonplace. An artist may on the other hand, wish to provide the viewer with a harmonious and peaceful impression and in this case the approach would be more calm and orderly. Whatever the desired response might be, its successful communication depends on the artist's control of the drawing and awareness of what is expected of it.

Expectations play a major role in most things which we do, and Art is no exception. However in many cases subjects and traditional expectations are handed down to the artist through the centuries. The nude figure, for example, has been a common subject in Art for thousands of years because of the 'ideal' it represents. In spite of this it continues to be controversial, which may be part of its appeal both for the artist and the viewer. The uninterrupted flow of the Lines and the Form presents a Visual harmony which is not duplicated by any other subject, making the nude figure a source of study of pure elements in Art. One could practice by drawing other subjects, and this is also important, but the life force of a figure is an essential element. Because the nude is a subject which is common and familiar, as well as 'ideal', it allows the artist freedom to experiment with various approaches or Visual Ideas.

Drawing the clothed figure to develop character and Expression is another form of traditional subject matter with expectations different from that of drawing the nude. Clothing is familiar and we relate to it as part of the model's personality. Here again the artist is presented with a subject, possibly in a classroom with a group of other people drawing the same model, where one does not have to seek out or think about what to use in the way of subject matter but is free to experiment with Abstract Concepts in drawing. Having subjects presented has advantages for that reason, but one must also independently seek out and discover one's own choice of Literal content for this more accurately reflects the interests and priorities of the artist.

Many subjects have served artists well over the years. These include still-life groups, landscapes, portraits, or bird and animal studies, and they give the artist opportunity to communicate through the familiarity of a traditional subject but interpreted in a personal manner. Artists have always tried to capture some of the wonder of Nature in their work and to share their impressions with others. A non-objective form of subject matter is a recent addition to the list of possibilities and is boundless and inexhaustible.

Whether a subject is personally inspiring or dictated does not guarantee a satisfactory work of Art. The work itself must inspire or relate to the viewer in some way. To produce a drawing which displays a Visual Idea must be the artist's dominant concern for the sake of one's sense of purpose and creativity. It must be kept in mind that the subject is only the Literal Meaning, and the artist must supply the Visual Meaning.

A drawing is expected to have some form of meaning. This is most often a balance of Literal and Visual qualities which attract the interest of the viewer. Beautiful handwriting is admired for the way it enhances a message which would otherwise be cold Information. Lines which are interesting to look at but carry no literal message must be presented in such a way that they possess a real 'meaning' through their apparent activity on the page. In this case they have to work harder, having no 'subject matter' to fall back on. The same applies to other non-objective situations where the artist must present his Idea in an understandable manner by heightening the role of the Abstract Concepts. A Shape having no familiar connotations must be presented as 'special' if it is to attract interest and evoke an emotional response. Textures and other Concepts must be developed to the point where no other subject is needed or wanted.

For successful communication of an Idea the artist must instill a real energy into the work. The viewer must also make the effort to share the experience and try to understand what the artist has created. One must be free to express his or her own Ideas, and the viewer must be free to accept or reject them.

Drawing Ideas develop as a reflection of the artist's interests and concerns. The need to express oneself visually combines with the enjoyment of doing the drawing and solving the problems which confront the artist with each new Idea. Drawing is a thinking process as well as a spontaneous one, and the two elements make up the prime ingredients of creativity. Drawing also enhances our appreciation of the world around us by involving us in an ongoing natural and creative activity. It is said that there is "nothing new under the sun", but in fact new things are continually being created, and that is the encouraging part.

Patty Hill

Dan Werstuk

160

Jane Everard

Monica Shelton

162

June Chambers

163

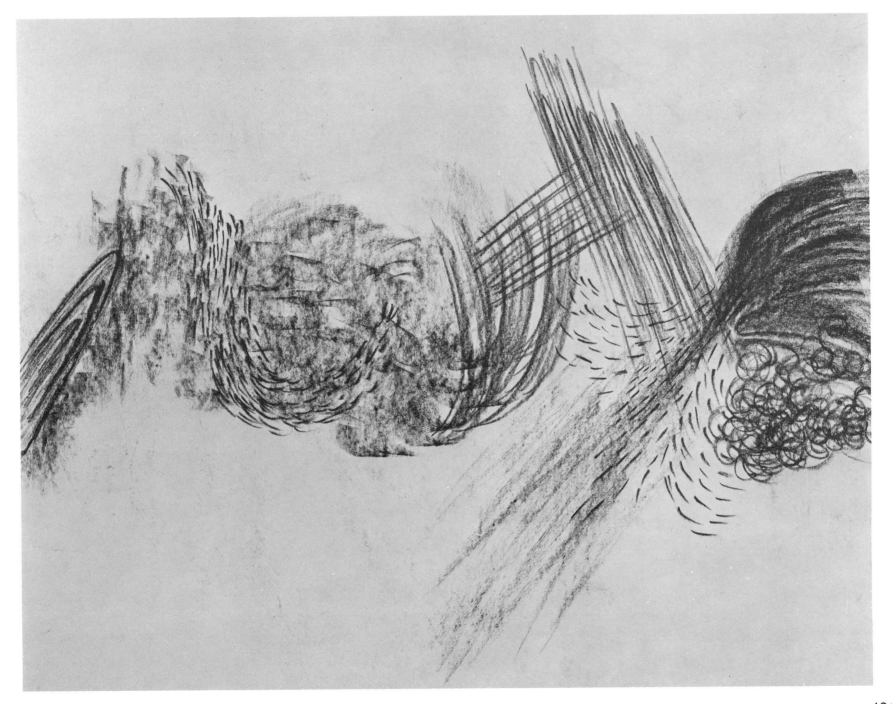

Michelle Orser   164

Marg Mayhew

Index

attraction 52-55, 139

Banner 74
Barker 21, 130
Benelow 23
Bonheur 137
Bonnard 141
Breughel 137, 141, 156

Carr 151
Cezanne 4, 99, 125, 141
Chambers 163
Clark-Thompson 105
Coburn 78, 129
color 2, 36, 67, 68, 71, 75, 76, 84, 126
Colville 141
composition 2, 4, 34, 36, 106, 119-142
Constable 126
contrast 97-100, 137, 139
control 3, 4, 5, 34, 115, 137
Curnoe 36, 111

Dali 99, 137, 141
Danby 156
Da Vinci 97, 123, 156
De Chirico 99
Dees 110
Dunbrook 80
Dunford 107, 109

Eckhardt 80
edge 57, 84, 125, 126
Everard 98, 121, 161
expression 2, 104, 106, 115, 145-152, 155, 156, 158

Fitzgerald 45
foreshortening 51-52
form 2, 4, 11, 34, 41-64, 67, 76, 83, 97, 115, 133, 137, 148, 151, 157
Fraser 17
Fung 150

Gadowski 32, 142
Gillham 33
Gottlieb 137
Goya 111, 133

harmony 133, 134
Harvey 93
Hill 150, 159
Hockney 16
Hoffman 26
Hopper 108, 151
Husband 19

idiom 155-166
information 2, 103-116, 134, 139, 148, 158

Jones 64

Kennedy 100
Kerslake 60
Kinsey 79
Kirk 113
Klee 11, 16, 36, 137, 146, 151, 156
Kollwitz 151
Kurelik 99, 151

light 43-46
line 2, 4, 7-24, 27, 28, 31, 36, 45, 46, 48, 53, 58, 67, 99, 108, 112, 125, 126, 128, 131, 133, 134, 139, 145, 146, 148, 157, 158

MacDonald 141
Machan 3, 9
Macmillan 10
Magritte 99, 137
Markan 118
Markle 156
Martin 61, 62, 77, 147
materials 4, 11, 12, 20, 27, 68, 106, 120, 125, 146
Matisse 4, 99
Mayhew 165
meaning, literal 1, 2, 7, 111, 133, 158; visual 1, 2, 3, 4, 5, 7, 34, 41, 99, 145, 158

Michelangelo 156
Milne 11
Miro 156
Modigliani 4, 34, 131
Mondrian 125, 141
Moore 58
Motherwell 125
Munch 151

nature 3, 8, 18, 28, 41, 52, 57, 58, 67, 71, 76, 83, 95, 97, 133, 137, 146, 158

Oldenburg 111
Ormiston 112
Orser 6, 164
Owen 35, 91

Penhale 59
perspective 2, 83-100
Pharand 14
Picasso 4, 11, 16, 36, 58, 126, 146, 151, 156
plane 46-49
Pratt 4

Redon 99
Rembrandt 11, 97, 126, 146, 156
repetition 128
rhythm 131
Robillard 38
Rothko 4, 126, 151

Scanlan 144
sculpture 58-64
Seurat 45, 75, 125
shape 2, 4, 7, 27-38, 41, 43, 45, 51, 57, 67, 68, 71, 76, 99, 104, 112, 115, 120, 123, 128, 131, 133, 134, 139, 145, 151, 158; negative and positive 31, 43, 45, 57, 71, 97, 103, 123, 125, 126, 128
Shelton 13, 37, 40, 42, 54, 73, 114, 122, 162
Snow 27
space 2, 51, 52, 53, 83-100, 108, 134, 137
structure 2, 4, 46, 119, 120, 125, 126, 128
subject 1, 2, 4, 15, 16, 20, 31, 34, 41, 43, 45, 52, 53, 97, 99, 103, 104, 106, 111, 112, 133, 137, 145, 148, 157, 158; nonobjective 4, 8, 20, 28, 45, 99, 104, 112, 119, 133, 137, 158

Taylor 30, 116
technique 3, 15, 68, 75, 76, 112, 133
tension 134-135, 139, 141
texture 2, 4, 11, 43, 67-80, 84, 106, 123, 133, 158
Tinkle 156
Turner 108, 156

Van Gogh 36, 75, 131, 146, 156
Vasarely 4, 119
Vermeer 45, 125, 156
viewer 2, 12, 16, 27, 52, 104, 128, 131, 133, 134, 139, 148, 157, 158

Warhol 141
Webster 10, 149
Werstuk 160
Whistler 4, 125
Wilson 4
Wyeth 4, 36, 99, 119, 125, 137, 141, 156